# THE SOCIAL REF

## How to Become a Better Referee and Umpire

*www.SocialRef.net*

*Great T's always come in 3's.*
*This book is for Toni, Tabitha and Tricia.*

# Contents

# The Worst Call of All Time.

What's the worst officiating call in the history of sports? Maybe you have a few ideas.

My college roommate Matt thought the worst call of all time was an illegal forward pass the refs called in his high school football championship, one that erased a game-winning touchdown throw. He often demonstrated–in our cramped freshman dorm room–how the QB jumped and threw the pass *before* he landed on the other side of the line of scrimmage.

Maybe he was a bit biased. . . he was the quarterback.

I'm watching football with my dad on a Sunday afternoon in 1998 when Vinny Testaverde, QB for the New York Jets, dives into the end zone on 4th down to score the game-winning touchdown. One problem: the football in his left hand never came close to crossing the goal-line; the refs only saw his helmet cross. That call was so bad that the NFL voted to bring back instant replay the next year.

In 2010, umpire Jim Joyce ruined the rarest of sports occurrences—a perfect game in baseball—by blowing a close call at first base with two outs in the ninth inning. Tigers pitcher Armando Galarraga had retired 26 batters in a row, only to see a historic moment taken from him at the last possible second. That call led to baseball using instant replay, too.

Two brothers watched Golden Tate's infamous "Fail Mary" end zone catch live and in person on a Monday night in Seattle in 2012. As soon as the replacement ref ruled a touchdown, the older brother turned to the younger one and said, *"We got this, there is no way they can overturn that call."* I was the older brother. A week later those replacement refs were gone.

These are all terrible calls. . . but not the worst.

The worst call of all time occurred during an NCAA football game in 1990 between Colorado and Missouri. Colorado trailed late, moved down the field, and after five straight goal-line plays, scored the game winning touchdown. The win gave them a share of the National Championship later that year.

If you're a football fan, you already know a team only gets 4 downs per series. The refs gave Colorado a $5^{th}$ down, and they scored a game-winning, national championship-affecting touchdown on that down.

That's my pick for the worst call of all time.

It wasn't the impact on the championship, or the time in the game it occurred, or even how embarrassing it was when the refs stayed on the field for 20 minutes after they'd realized their mistake, trying to figure out what to do, before finally giving up.

Matt the roommate's illegal forward pass, Vinny's Helmet, Jim and Armando and the "almost perfect" game, the confused rulings of crappy replacement NFL refs–those were all calls of judgment.

There is no judgment involved in the awarding of a $5^{th}$ down, just a breakdown in a system you control. There were at least six refs on that field. Did any of them feel something off? Did one of them *know* something was wrong but was afraid to speak up or stop the game? Did they all just follow along during the worst call of all time?

Maybe this sort of thing is just a once in a life-time mistake. Except it has happened multiple times, before and since.

In a 1940 college football game between Cornell and Dartmouth, Cornell won 7-3 on a last second touchdown, on a $5^{th}$ down mistakenly awarded by the refs. They at least forfeited the game later, once they realized what happened.

The Miami Hurricanes won a college football game in 1972 with a $5^{th}$ down touchdown. In a 1968 NFL game, a team only got 3 downs on a pivotal drive.

How many more times has this happened, and no one even noticed?

We can guarantee it will happen tomorrow night. . . on a flag football field somewhere across the country: someone will get a $5^{th}$ down, or only 3 downs. Or it will be a missing point, a lost minute, an extra timeout that didn't exist—maybe even a score written down backwards after a great game.

It will happen. . . but will anyone notice? Will you notice? *Will you be involved?*

Players and fans that don't like a ref's judgment may complain of bias or about 'being cheated'. In truth, in recreational, youth, and intramural sports leagues across the country, players and teams *do* get cheated every day.

They get cheated out of their game information: Time, runs, outs, innings, downs, goals and even timeouts.

**This happens because the main way recreational refs and umps are trained and educated is wrong.**

As founder of Underdog Sports Leagues, an adult rec league in Seattle and Portland, I was wrong for over 10 years, as a ref and ump, and as a trainer.

I thought knowing the rulebook and getting the call correct every time was the key to being a great rec ref. As long as you got the call correct, the truth would shine through. If players didn't like my call: tough crap. If they didn't understand my call, that just meant I had to repeat it louder.

If someone dared to attack my calls or insult me personally, well look out. In those days I always had an arrow dripping with sarcasm, ready to fire right back.

Problem players needed to be flagged, scolded, and ejected, or else I would lose respect and become a "push over".

When Underdog trained in new refs, I would spend three hours reading through each line of the rulebook with them. When things got busier, we put the process on video—just me standing up against the wall, still reading and talking through the rulebook for three hours.

When a new ref was struggling, I would stand behind them at the field whispering in their ear the penalties and calls they should make in real time, thinking that would help them become a "stronger" ref.

I taught the wrong way because I learned the wrong way, because almost every program teaches the wrong way: get the rules memorized, get the calls correct, act like a pro, keep your composure, and everything else will just "work out."

The rulebook will tell you there are four downs a series. It will never tell you:

> How do you keep track of the downs?
>
> How often should you announce them?
>
> What should you do when you say its $2^{nd}$ down and player thinks its $3^{rd}$?
>
> **How do you build systems and habits to make sure a team never gets a $5^{th}$ Down?**

When I notched a few hundred games as a ref, and stopped worrying about arguments, and conflict, and people saying mean stuff about me, I noticed something:

The best, most well-liked, and longest-lasting referees in our program were great communicators first. They started with things they could control, like game info, and built trust and credibility with players through clear communication.

They had a simple priority: First, they got the game info right.

They became more than just regular officials—they became **Social Refs**: masters in communicating game info, defusing conflict, and positive, proactive game control.

They over-communicated the most boring stuff, like the down and distance in a flag football game. They loved helping and teaching players. They loved joking around. They took the old script of the angry ump–always battling with the players–and flipped it on its head. Players loved these officials so much, they would come back season after season BECAUSE of the refs!

Jay from Montana had never reffed a game before in his life when he sat across from us in his interview. Ten years later when he came in to the office to try and retire, we looked up his career stats: eight thousand games across flag football, softball, kickball, dodgeball, and even some bowling and mini-golf.

He had become a teacher, a friend, and the best Social Ref I had ever seen.

*Jay and his signature smile at a kickball game*

Jay is a hero, because he taught us the most important lesson, the one that many refs never learn:

**KEY CONCEPT**

### It's not the calls, it's YOUR communication.

The purpose of this book is to help build a communication system you can use for any rec sport or league, and to identify and defeat the instincts and habits in your brain right now that will work against your success.

If you think back to our 5th down play, it's not a "call" at all; just bad communication. The refs didn't call a charge a blocking foul, or catch an incompletion, or call a runner safe when she was actually out. They simply let the game run on its own, with incorrect information, and didn't speak up or step in to stop a small issue from becoming a legend.

To communicate with people who are passionate about sports, you need a system. The players may change, but a system will get you through the tough calls, close plays, and hard games that wreck many new refs.

**In tough games, refs with a system can level up, refs without a plan will give up.**

The ability to create fun, build credibility, and avoid arguments and melt-downs seldom comes down to what you say. It's always more about the timing and delivery of how you say it.

Maybe you are here because you love sports and just need a part time job. That's where most beginning refs start. But maybe you really want to learn how to make better decisions, how to communicate under pressure, and how to step up and lead when things feel like they are going in the wrong direction.

Maybe in the past when you were misunderstood, disrespected, or ignored by others, you got louder and angrier, more sarcastic, and kept repeating yourself. I certainly tried this method.

**Can you turn off these old habits and instincts, and create new communication habits of a Social Ref?**

I don't know your league format or rules, but in building your new system, I know where to start:

Communication.

The rules don't change, but you can. If you are misunderstood, shy, anti-social—even if you are bad at sports—you can still become a great rec referee, just like Jay and so many others, if you start with simple communication.

As a rec ref you are going to have to tell people things they won't like, and things they don't want to hear.

What system will you use to give good people bad news?

Players and people in life will say, *"You're wrong,"* and demand you change your mind, and switch your calls. First change your instincts and communication habits. Then you will be able to succeed where so many others have stumbled.

If you want to be a better official, a more confident teacher, and maybe even a better leader and communicator in your daily life, come along and let's get started on your journey to becoming a Social Ref.

# The Two Brains

Your brain is full of instincts, short-cuts, and communication habits you have formed while trying to solve problems, get better at things, avoid mistakes, and deal with conflict in life. We'll call this your **Beginner Brain**. It seems to be in good working order–you've read this far–but it will make it very hard for you to become a great rec ref . . . unless we can start making changes.

Why?

The **Beginner Brain** is emotional, impulsive, distracted, and quick to create problems. It's both a villain and a con-artist that loves complexity and confusion. It steals your attention and energy to use on problems that don't matter. It tricks you and says, 'do what is easy, do what feels good in the moment'. On your Social Ref journey, you will need to defeat this "villain" one idea and habit at a time.

If you show up to your first shift with your Beginner Brain still running things, you will spend a lot of time and energy on the wrong problems:

> *What if I make the wrong call?*
>
> *What if I forget a rule or signal?*
>
> *What if people don't see me as tough enough? What if they don't respect me?*

*What snappy comeback can I use to put someone in their place when they argue?*

These questions will all feel like huge issues at first. In the big picture, they really aren't very important; just normal tricks from your **Beginner Brain**.

The **Ref Brain** is methodical, consistent, detached, and focused on what is truly important. This is the brain of a Social Ref.

Social Refs are great communicators. They don't leave things to chance. They don't guess, or wait to see how things play out. They never make themselves the center of attention. They own the game, and its many responsibilities, while still fading into the background.

Every great ref succeeds because they have built a **communication system** that works, whatever the sport or league. Their system allows them to handle the many parts of the job simultaneously. The system is a combination of core habits, instincts, skills, and philosophy that help you operate in Ref Brain mode.

The aim of this book is to get you started with the foundation of that system. We will provide you with tools and **Simple Starts**, and help you avoid the traps and tricks your Beginner Brain says are okay.

We hope to build these **5 Key Habits** that *every* Social Ref uses *every* game:

> **Habit #1**: Climb Down off the Pedestal
> **Habit #2**: See the Third Game
> **Habit #3**: Become the Scoreboard
> **Habit #4**: Become a Defuser
> **Habit #5**: Change the Future

To truly build these habits, we need to switch the settings in your brain–one at a time–from Beginner Brain settings to Ref Brain settings.

Beginner Brain habits, instincts, and impulses (switches set to the left) are normally bad and normally a trap when reffing. Through practice and experience, we want to create new habits and instincts, flipping

# The Social Ref Switchboard™

**Phase 1: DECIDE** ⊶ Key Habit: Climb Down Off The Pedestal

**CAP SWITCH**

Lesson Reps | Growth Reps

**OVER-REF SWITCH**

Outliers & Procedures | Obvious & Important

**TURTLE SWITCH**

Hide Behind Rules & Gear | Hide Behind Info & Hustle

**Phase 2: LEARN & TRAIN** ⊶ Key Habit: See The Third Game

**SPECTATOR SWITCH**

TV Ball | Ref Ball

**CONNECTION SWITCH**

Some Plays Some Time | Every Play All The Time

**DECISION SWITCH**

Stop & Think | Move To Decide

**Phase 3: SURVIVE** *(0-15 Games)* ⊶ Key Habit: Become The Scoreboard

**FREQUENCY SWITCH**

1 And Done | 3-Rep Communication

**CUSTOMER SERVICE SWITCH**

Respond To Everything | Answer What Matters

**REF BIG SWITCH**

Ref Big When Easy | Ref Big When Close

**HABIT SWITCH**

Remember Habit | Universal Habit/Solution

# www.socialref.net

PRACTICE DIALS

WALK /RUN BACKWARDS · PRACTICE SCRIPTS · REF-JOURNAL WORK · SIGNALS AND CCS · WARNINGS & DEFUSERS · "RUDDER" PHRASES

**Phase 4: STABILIZE** *(15-50 Games)* Key Habit: Become A Defuser

TMI SWITCH
Over-Explain Calls | Over-Explain Game Info

PERSPECTIVE SWITCH
Here's What You Did | Here's What I Saw

SIMPLE TALK SWITCH
Classroom Talk | Field Talk

COMEBACK SWITCH
Say What Feels Good | Avoid Instant Comebacks

DEFUSER SWITCH
Try To Win & Change Minds | Defuse & Pivot

**Phase 5: DRIVE & THRIVE** *(50 Games+)* Key Habit: Change The Future

PROACTIVE SWITCH
Wait & Watch | Default To Action

WARNING SWITCH
Negative & Scolding | Opportunity To Teach, Connect

ACCOUNTABILITY SWITCH
It's The Players | It's My System

⚫ **STOP AND SQUASH BUGS** ⚫

RE-ENACT · 100% QUALIFIERS · POINTING OUT · SHAKING NO'S · LOOK AROUND

the switches to the right side and into Ref Brain mode. The more switches you flip, the more you activate your Ref Brain.

These switches are not set in stone. You can make progress, and they can easily flip back. Nothing works every time. As you build and solidify a system, you will recognize when you have slipped back into Beginner Brain mode.

We will learn about the Key Habits and their switches by moving through 5 phases of ref development:

> **Phase 1**: Decide
> **Phase 2**: Learn and Train
> **Phase 3**: Survive (0-15 games)
> **Phase 4**: Stabilize (15-50 games)
> **Phase 5**: Drive (50+ games)

Moving through each phase while learning its key habit and switches will help build a system you own.

As one of my favorite mentors, Jim Rohn, used to say: *"You can't hire someone else to do your push-ups for you."*

You have to work on your Beginner Brain in order to get better as a ref. We can't make the calls or build the system for you. It has to be one you build and create, because it's your brain!

# Scouting Report

This book will help new refs and umps in a **"rec league"** setting the most. Youth leagues, church and gym leagues, college intramural programs, parks and rec leagues, and adult sports leagues like Underdog are all rec leagues.

"Refs" includes referees, umpires, supervisors, line judges, and any other rec officials — it's just simpler to call everyone a "ref", regardless of the sport we discuss (we'll use the terms 'ref,' 'ump,' and 'official' interchangeably). Anyone can grab a whistle and jersey and be a ref. We want to help you build a communication system that allows you to join a special club of **Social Refs.**

First, you need to "Survive". If you are reffing your first game in two hours, and you have no clue what you are doing, read your rule book twice (standing up) and then read "Phase 2" and "Phase 3" of this book. These are the basics to get you through your first few games. Later in the book, we'll discuss ideas and tools to help you thrive and continue to improve your switchboard.

The default assumptions and ideas you have about reffing in your Beginner Brain are **"Ref Myths"**. Some ideas we share will go against these "Ref Myths", so you may have to trust our **"Ref Truths"** first, before you get a chance to experience them in real time.

REF MYTH

The main tool that will get us to our "Ref Truths" and a new communication system is the brain switchboard introduced in the previous section. We will discuss key concepts, practice techniques, simple starting points, personal experience, and stories from the field, all with the goal of flipping your switches from Beginner Brain to Ref Brain mode.

We also have a couple more brain ideas:

**Reversal Ideas:** You already have this idea in your head, but you need to see it from the opposite direction.

REVERSAL

**Stop & Squash Bugs**: Even a good system has the occasional bug. Stop and Squash these bugs—no movement or reversal—just get rid of them as fast as possible.

STOP & SQUASH

We'll introduce big concepts from my personal mentors outside of the sports world. And I'll use some movie lines, corny jokes, Bruce Lee quotes, and icons to help us along:

My background is strongest in flag football, softball and kickball—with some basketball, dodgeball, and soccer mixed in—so those will be the examples I reference the most. Even if your sport or rules system isn't mentioned here, the communication ideas and tools we teach can be used for almost every sport, because communication with players is actually predictable and similar. You are smart enough to adapt an idea from a kickball story, even if you never ump a game of kickball in your life.

I have never met you, but I believe you can be a great ref—otherwise I wouldn't have spent so much f*cking time writing this book! I have made all the mistakes for you, and tried to simplify things into 5 key Social Ref habits that I wish I understood 18 years ago.

I'm a somewhat private person. I spent most of high school hiding in my room playing video games and messing with my modem. I didn't have my first kiss until I was 19. Even today, when I go to give a speech, I get a big pimple on the end of my nose that hurts like hell. But it reminds me of a key ref habit . . . stay humble.

You can do this, because I did it, and Jay did it, and hundreds of others have done it as well.

Don't waste time criticizing and yelling at refs on television if you've never been in their shoes. Don't waste years trying to learn how to ref through trial and error. Spend two hours learning how to communicate, and build a system that avoids the instincts and traps that don't work, to be a better ref.

Some of the more visual lessons of the book, like body language and signals, have online videos and courses you can find at **socialref.net**.

If you want to ask advice, or share a success story, drop me an email at **shawn@socialref.net**. We often speak at universities and consult with other sports leagues, if you think these ideas can help your program and staff.

If you are a brand new ref, and email a selfie celebrating your first game, I will send you back a small gift!

Let's go.

# KEY HABIT: CLIMB DOWN OFF THE PEDESTAL

### The Chess "Lesson"

*Miami, Fl, 1992:* Mr. Coats—the high school basketball coach and my summer school PE and Health teacher—makes a surprising offer on the first day of class:

> *"If any of you play chess after class is over and beat me, I will give you an A for the course and you don't have to come back for the rest of the semester."*

I had a feeling this wasn't the first time Coach Coats made this offer, but I loved chess and hated summer school, so what was the downside?

The downside was that Coach Coats was really good at chess.

The first few weeks were awful. I sucked; even with my friend Tim rooting me on, I lost and lost and lost again. Then I actually got better. I learned Coach Coats's habits and preferences, where he liked to move. I lost . . . slower.

Then one game it happened: I thought, '*hey, I might actually have a chance here.*' Apparently, Coach Coats saw it, too, because he used a move I had never seen before: an *en passant*, the only move in chess that allows you to take a piece without actually landing on the space. In certain *very special* cases, you can take someone else's pawn just by passing by it with your pawn.

"What the crap Coach? Pawns can't move sideways!" was about all I could say.

I was confused, and angry, and it just *felt* wrong.

Coach Coats began a long lecture to prove pawns could move in this super-secret special way. He pulled out old books. He showed me his certificate with title as a special chess "master," or something I had also never heard of before.

Coach may have felt like he was **teaching**, but really all he was doing was **explaining**:

> Explaining why he was smarter.
> Explaining that he had more experience.
> Explaining how he was correct, and how I just needed to learn the rule.

Beginner Brain explanations are like this—they all sound the same to players:

**Let me explain why I am right, and you are wrong.**

From the very first play, you start on a pedestal. You have that special uniform, and training, and knowledge. You have tools, equipment, and vocabulary. You've read special books and passed special tests. You don't dress or act or move or talk like anyone else on the field.

All this reinforces the natural distance between officials and players. Your Beginner Brain tricks you into thinking that distance *should* be there and that the pedestal is where you belong—just EXPLAIN to the world what you know and think, and everything else will be fine.

Refs have **power**—the power to take away points, to wipe out plays, and sometimes to even kick you out of the game. Even more distance.

So the first habit of a Social Ref is:

Every chance you get, climb down off this pedestal of power, and meet the players where they are. Always shrink the distance.

 **Nobody came to watch you ref.**

KEY CONCEPT

It's not about you. It's about the game, and the players in the game.

New refs are so defensive—so scared of making the wrong call and being questioned—that they instinctively raise the pedestal without even thinking.

You hear it in common phrases:

> *"I know the rules better than you do."*
> *"I'm the ref, and I make the calls."*
> *"I'm in charge here, just let me do my job."*

**If you have to say you are in charge, you aren't in charge, you're just acting like a jerk.**

**KEY CONCEPT**

You *should* know the rules better than 95% of the players on the field. You *should* be able to see things that most normal players and fans will miss. Will you act that way?

Will you lean on your title, certificates, and power, and magnify the distance between you and the players?

Do you need to always be right? To prove your point? To "win" every argument?

You will end up being the most "right" referee that no one wants anywhere near their game.

A soccer game, or a chess game.

The best refs understand this idea, and climb down off the pedestal as much as possible.

They don't throw titles and power in someone's face.

They don't cite obscure rules and names that only they would know about. (*en passants*)

They don't act like a boss or parent and lecture and scold people.

And they stay humble. They fade into the background of the game and let the players shine.

After my eventual loss that day, I never played chess against Coach Coats again that Summer. In fact, I didn't play chess at all for almost 10 more years.

All because Coach Coats "couldn't climb down off the pedestal."

All because of one rule that was obvious to "an expert", and brand new to a "casual player" like me.

We call the first phase, **Decide** because you decide to take the job, but you also decide WHY you want to ref. Need cash? Love sports? Want to be the boss, because maybe you are always bossed around? Do you want to be up on that pedestal? Be honest about your reasons, because building a solid system will take real work and practice.

Nobody likes to lose, but people will play as long as they feel the game is safe, fair and fun.

I was fine losing to Coach Coats over and over again, until he made me feel like a loser.

It wasn't the rule, it was the communication.

You will have many "Coach Coats" moments in your reffing career. Decide how you will respond when you know and understand more than players. Whenever you can. . . climb down off the pedestal, close the distance, and stay humble.

# Meet CAP

Before you even step on the field, you need to meet and understand **CAP**, destroyer of new refs:

> C—Conflict
> A—Adversity
> P—Passion

## Conflict is built into the DNA of the job.

**KEY CONCEPT**

Refs call penalties and fouls, throw flags, pull out yellow and red cards, take away catches and plays and points, and even yell that a player is "OUT!" at the top of their lungs.

Ask yourself:

> Do *you* like it when you get called out for mistakes in front of friends and co-workers?

> Do *you* enjoy getting criticized by people with more power and control than you?

> Do *you* like messing up, being confused, and not getting a second chance to fix things?

Nobody does. So **Conflict**—the C in CAP—is a given. You have to work to erase the built-in conflict people expect when you put on that uniform.

**Adversity** kicks in when you add more ingredients to the conflict: multiple people yelling at you, field problems, bad weather, and the idea that often the better you do your job, **the harder it becomes**.

At most jobs, you get compliments or a pat on the back for doing things "by the book." In reffing, you will make a great call that is 100% correct. . . only to have an entire team yelling at you and hating your guts. Like a police officer handing out speeding tickets, the better you do your job, the more conflict, the more adversity, the more "REF, YOU SUCK!" comments you can expect. Fun stuff.

The **Passion** in CAP comes from the players, from their desire to play well, and to **WIN**.

A new ref thinks a rec league is some laid-back deal with a bunch of amateur players, but most players have been living, watching, and playing sports their whole lives. They may not have the skill of the pros, but they have no shortage of PASSION. They don't play because they have to, but because they really love it!

**REF MYTH**

**Ref Myth:** *It's just goofy rec sports.* Players don't care if they win or lose, they "just want to play and have fun."

**Ref Truth:** As long as there is a game, and a scoreboard, **people want to win**. There is Conflict and Adversity and Passion because people like winning!

Once upon a time, Underdog tried to run a kickball league where winning didn't matter. There was no official score; teams got awarded points for spirit and costumes. I thought it was the most brilliant idea of all time.

**Everyone hated it.** The people we thought would like it hated it. Even the people who thought *they* would like it, hated it. We canceled it after two seasons.

We tried to build a "just for fun" league where CAP could not exist, and scores didn't matter, and it didn't work. People want to win, feel good, and play well, even when they say out loud that it doesn't matter.

I am a volunteer ref for a youth basketball league at the local rec center. These games don't keep score either, I ref for free, and the players are all seven years old. I don't get any conflict from the kids, but we *still* have multiple CAP moments with adult coaches and fans who think I made a bad call and need to tell me about it.

Because reffing is **a lot like politics**.

People will ignore truth and facts and instead argue with your call based on how they FEEL about it. There is no **absolute truth** on the field; just perspectives.

Players will argue the easiest call with responses and stories that make no sense, and leave you like Will Ferrell in Zoolander, screaming internally "I FEEL LIKE I'M TAKING CRAZY PILLS!" These responses come from passion.

People *feel* your calls way before they understand or agree with them.

If a player loves the game with a **passion**, and *feels* like you are getting in the way of that, get ready for more CAP, regardless of the stakes of the game or the skill levels involved.

Never assume you know the players. You don't know how far they drove to play, how bad their day was, how things are going in their personal life, and how much of their identity is wrapped up in a game.

**People don't get mad about rules, they get mad about how the rules are enforced.**

CAP *will* find you on the field. The question is: How will you respond the first time you encounter it?

# Lesson and Growth Reps

CAP brings us to our first brain switch. Remember we want to switch our brain instincts from left (Beginner Brain), to right (Ref Brain).

When you encounter CAP for the first time should you:

**Attack it head on (fight response)?**

**Or run away from it as fast as possible (flight response)?**

Both paths are a mistake.

Fighting CAP head on is a bad idea; it puts you right back on the pedestal and. . . creates more CAP! We will talk later about specific ways to defuse CAP with one of the Key Habits (Become a Defuser).

Running away is an even worse idea, so let's tackle that now before it infects your system early.

**Scenario:**

> *It's the last minute of your second flag football game ever, and you see the most obvious Pass Interference call: the defender lands on the receiver's shoulders and back before the ball arrives. This feels like your first really BIG call. You were a little hesitant, a little timid earlier, but this is a no doubter! By the book! This is what they pay you 12 bucks an hour for! Let's do this, penalty flag!*

Your pride and happiness last the time it takes the flag to hit the ground. That's when you get responses like this:

> **WHAT THE F\*CK REF! HOW IN THE HELL CAN YOU MAKE THAT CALL ???**
>
> **ARE YOU KIDDING ME? YOU MAKE THAT CALL NOW AND NOT WHEN I GOT TACKLED IN THE ENDZONE??**
>
> **HOW WERE YOU EVEN CLOSE ENOUGH TO SEE THAT???**
>
> **I HAVE A RIGHT TO GO FOR THAT BALL! ARE YOU TRYING TO GIVE THEM THE GAME???**

Welcome to reffing! Were these potential responses not mentioned in your rulebook?

Another ref runs up and asks what the flag was for.

> *"Defensive pass interference. . . I think. Uhhhh maybe. I'm not sure. . . what did you see? Should I have thrown that? Was that a mistake?"*

(BTW: New refs say this out loud with every player watching and listening.)

You made the right call, the call you were supposed to make. The problem is your body and your brain HATED the results: getting yelled at, attacked, and insulted.

Your Beginner Brain says: *"Man, that felt like crap! How can I avoid that stress and conflict again?"*

It tricks you into seeing player conflict as a lesson:

> *"That was a bad experience, and we learned a lesson.
> The lesson is: Let's never try that again."*

Some **Lesson Reps** are vital: You touch a hot stove as a kid, burn your hand, and learn never to do it again (You can almost hear mom: *"I hope you learned your lesson. . . "*)

Other times we confuse an opportunity to get better—a **Growth Rep**—with a **Lesson Rep** and learn the wrong lesson: You try stand-up comedy for the first time ever at an open mic, the response is underwhelming, so you decide: *"That was a mistake. I'll never try that again. . ."*

The WORST thing you can do in your first few games is let your Beginner Brain take over and do what it naturally wants to do: file that first big CAP call as a Lesson Rep, with the lesson being, **let's never put ourselves in that situation again.** The BEST thing you can do is see the situation as a Growth Rep: It sucks right now, but in going through it, your system will get better, and you will come out stronger.

The first time you fell off your bike and skinned your knee, the response was probably, *"I need to get better,"* instead of *"I am never going to touch a bike ever again!"*

Converting conflict into Lesson Reps teaches you to run away from CAP, to hide from the big calls. You 'fade away' from even the basic rulings you must make—safe or out, fair or foul—because you are trying to hide from CAP. You ref small in the biggest moments, hoping that somehow CAP won't find you.

Then, you don't make the big obvious and important calls a ref needs to make, and instead find smaller, less controversial stuff to focus on—procedures and policies where everything is black and white and there is no chance for arguments—and you **Over-Ref** on those.

In a rec league, when you "go looking" for calls to make, you will never run out of material.

OVER-REF SWITCH

Outliers & Procedures    Obvious & Important

Changing a call because of CAP would be bad, but changing your system, and teaching your brain to avoid CAP because your great call feels like a big mistake is even worse. Your Beginner Brain will keep your Over-Ref Switch stuck in the safe zone of Outliers & Procedures, instead of the important rulings and calls.

**Everyone notices when a ref is stuck on the smallest calls, because they are afraid of the big ones.**

CAP is a given. The bigger the call, the bigger the CAP.

We start with CAP—even before rules and game info—because if you let your brain turn normal CAP experiences into Lesson Reps, you will be lost before you even get started.

# The Bias

Nick, one of our Hall of Fame Social Refs, says it best:

 **Are players questioning you, or asking a question?**

**KEY CONCEPT**

Beginning refs don't understand CAP, and don't know how to respond to it. So they take it personally, and question themselves.

*"Did I screw that up?"*

**CAP may feel like crap, but it's not about you.**

If you see CAP as an attack, instead of a normal human response, then you start to see everything as an attack.

Every comment feels like a criticism.

Every question feels like an arrow.

The psychology that explains why you shouldn't take any of this personally, no matter how personal it *feels*, is the idea of **Self-Serving Bias**: the brain has a natural instinct to give itself credit for wins and accomplishments, and assign blame to others for losses and failures.

> *I did really well on the final exam because I am smart, but I did bad on my calculus final exam because the teacher made a poor test that was unfair.*

Or how about:

> *We won the championship because of great plays and our talent, but we lost BECAUSE OF THOSE SUCKY REFEREES!*

Half of the teams will probably use the defense mechanism of Self-Serving Bias and attack you, because half the teams will leave the court or field feeling like "losers". . . BECAUSE THEY JUST LOST!!

New refs encounter CAP and "The Bias," blame themselves, and **"turtle up."** They start hiding. They are still on the field, making the easy calls, but they are really hiding.

**TURTLE SWITCH**

Everyone hides when they first start reffing, because you're totally new! You can hide behind positive ideas like info and effort. Or you can hide in your turtle shell and listen to the Beginner Brain villain that says:

> *"It's better to do nothing next time a tough call comes up. If we keep our head down, maybe people won't get so angry and accuse us of being wrong!"*

Self Serving Bias says people **are guaranteed to say you are wrong**.

What a relief! We got that out of the way early!

Winners talk about the plays they made. . . losers talk about the refs.

You are going to get blamed for everything, even when you do a great job, even before you make your first mistake—and there will be plenty of mistakes.

This is part of "deciding" to become a ref. We don't want to scare you, just prepare you.

Don't hide from CAP and growth reps. Don't hide behind tiny calls and rules. Avoid becoming a "turtle". Go make the big calls and decisions your league needs.

## INTRO AND PHASE 1 RECAP

### KEY IDEAS

· It's not the calls that will make you great, it's your communication.

· Conflict is built into the job because **CAP** never cares if you are right or wrong. New refs want to run and hide from CAP, or fight it head on. Try and avoid doing both.

· When in doubt, climb down off the pedestal and stay humble. Avoid throwing titles, experience, and rules in people's faces.

· Your Beginner Brain is a villain. It is quick, complicated, and emotional, and tries to fool you into thinking you don't need a system, because everything is instant and easy.

· Flip the switches in each phase of your development to master the 5 Key Habits and turn on your Ref Brain, where things are deliberate, simple, logical, and based on habits you create.

- Don't confuse explaining with teaching. Explaining often comes off as a form of "let me tell you why I am right and you are wrong."

- Self-Serving Bias tells us that players give themselves credit when things go well, and tend to blame others, like the refs, when things go badly.

- Don't turn CAP from a great call into a Lesson Rep that makes it feel like a mistake. Make sure you treat experience from CAP like a Growth Rep.

**Phase 1: DECIDE**     🗝 Key Habit: Climb Down Off The Pedestal

**CAP SWITCH**
Lesson Reps — Growth Reps

**OVER-REF SWITCH**
Outliers & Procedures — Obvious & Important

**TURTLE SWITCH**
Hide Behind Rules & Gear — Hide Behind Info & Hustle

## PRACTICE

Identify examples of Self-Serving Bias in your daily experiences.

Start noticing CAP at school or work, where certain situations create automatic conflict.

Think through times in life when you slowed your progress by treating a learning opportunity like a hot stove lesson rep.

# KEY HABIT—SEE THE THIRD GAME

## The 3 Games

*Princeton NJ, 1951*—An undefeated Princeton college football team squares off against Dartmouth in what every newspaper describes as a brutal game. Tons of penalties are called. Princeton's star quarterback suffers a broken nose; a short time later Dartmouth's quarterback ends up with a broken leg! The game is written and talked about long after it's over, but two scientists, Hastorf and Cantril, don't care about the score as much as people's perceptions of the game.

They show game film to students from both schools and ask them a simple question:

> *"Who started it?"*

Their paper on the study, "They Saw a Game," shows how people can watch the same game, and still see things very differently.

Basically, the students from each school were "Homers"—they had wildly different opinions on the rough play in the game and who was at fault. Even when Dartmouth students admitted their team had been rough, many thought it was fair because, well, *Princeton started it first.*

Cantril and Hastorf describe a concept that took me years to understand and is the foundation of the second Key Habit:

There is never really one game. There are always many games within a game, because people see what they want to see and what makes sense to them.

**KEY CONCEPT**

**There are at least 3 versions of a game:**

The **First Game** the home team and their fans see.

The **Second Game** the away team and their fans see.

And the **THIRD GAME** that you as the ref need to see to do your job!

# The Three Training Switches

Beginning refs have trouble managing and reffing the Third Game because **they have trouble even seeing it**. They are watching the game, just the wrong version of it. They are watching the version that you would see on TV.

Even if you have never reffed a game in your life, you have likely played sports, and more importantly, watched sports on TV.

**REF MYTH**

**Ref Myth**: Watching lots of TV sports makes it easier to learn how to ref!

**Ref Truth**: Watching sports on TV teaches you to focus on the wrong things

The TV camera is always focused on the **ball**—where is it, who has it, where is it going. The camera follows the ball in the air on a deep pass downfield to the wide receiver. It follows the ball as it jumps off the bat, is kicked to mid-field by the goalie, or is chucked up for a last second 3-pointer. Watching sports on TV trains you to follow the ball like a dog watching a piece of steak.

**KEY CONCEPT**

**If you're watching the ball fly through the air, you are normally watching the wrong thing.**

To survive your first 15 games, you'll need to switch your Beginner's Brain from seeing the ball (TV Ball) to seeing the Third Game (Ref Ball).

Try to understand—there will be many times where the ball is crucial:

> *Did the ball break the plane of the end zone?*
>
> *Was the ball caught or trapped on the ground?*
>
> *Did the ball bounce off a player?*
>
> *Did the ball land fair or foul?*

Great refs train their brain to look for the ball LAST instead of first. They start with a whole different vantage point.

When the ball is in the air towards the left field foul line, a good ump positions herself on the line, not watching the ball.

A ref watches the receiver and defender run down field, not the ball in the air.

A ref watches two players fighting for position in the post, not the arc of the ball going towards the basket.

If you focus only on the ball, you will never have a chance to see the Third Game.

You can break this habit—and flip the spectator switch—with two simple starts:

**SIMPLE START**

**Think about "feet first".** Your instincts will be to watch the ball, or when someone doesn't have the ball, to watch their face and then "scroll down." The problem is that by the time you scroll down, you might miss the most important part of a play.

Social Refs normally start with the feet and scroll up to the hands and waist and finish with the face.

Start with the feet and look up. The ball will come into play.

Try it in your normal day-to-day: When someone comes into a room, start by noticing their shoes first. It might help you with compliments, and it will definitely help you as a ref.

**Start "looking off-ball".** You can't change the camera angles on TV, but you can watch live sports in a different way. The next time you go to a live game, try watching all the players who don't have the ball. Watch the refs, and watch what they are watching. Avoid following the pitcher or quarterback or point guard on every play; instead try watching everyone else except the person who starts the play with the game ball.

It might seem disorienting at first, but the ball will naturally come into play. You will start to get a feel for where it's going.

All the players in the first two games care about is **the ball**, but you need to see everything: the lines, the feet, the hands, the arms, the bases, and your surroundings.

Maybe the biggest reason a player hates your call is because they simply didn't see what you saw. Your Ref Brain starts watching a different game: the Third Game.

The first few times this happened in a game, I jokingly called it The Neo Principle—from Neo in *The Matrix*. By the end of the movie and his hero's journey, Neo (Keanu Reeves) sees the real world much differently than everyone else—he sees the green code of the Matrix that no one else can see.

After seeing this concept a few hundred times, it's no joke. When you see the Third Game, you will feel additional Adversity from CAP because, like Neo, you will begin to notice things that no one else can see.

Two players run down the center of the field, stride-for-stride. One grabs and pulls the other's jersey while the ball is in the air. You throw your flag for pass interference (grabbing the jersey is a common call across all sports—an action many players do automatically without even thinking). The ball arrives, and your call is already made, but the player who pulled the jersey holds their hands up in the universal *"I know I'm guilty but I swear I didn't really do anything"* pose.

Everyone else on the field was watching the ball; you were "looking off-ball."

The Neo Principle says that calls you make that only you can see will be **auto-arguments**: a call or decision *guaranteed* to be argued. Your call will generate a lot of CAP, not just from the player involved, but from EVERYONE on their team who was watching the First Game and following the ball. It's tough to be the hero and make a Neo Principle call, but you will see them when you start watching the Third Game.

As a player in the first two games, you normally get plays off. You sub out. You slow down a bit when the game is not on your part of the field. You play on offense and cheer and watch when the defense is on the field. You sit in the dugout in Softball or Baseball, and wait your turn to bat.

You can hyper-focus on the player in front of you–*all I have to do is stop them from scoring*–or a specific task: get this ball in play, defend this part of the field.

In the Third Game, there are no plays off. As a ref, you have to keep track of all the players, from both teams. You have to see huge parts of the field, sometimes the entire field.

You have to watch the offense and defense, the good plays and the bad plays. You don't get to sit in the dugout, and you don't get to sub out. If you focus on just one player, especially the star player with the ball, you will miss the Third Game.

Next time you play a sport, notice how often you don't finish the full play, or aren't even involved. You're standing in right field with your hands on your hips as your team records 3 outs in the infield. Your QB throws a long pass downfield and everyone else stops running. Your star point guard goes one-on-one and everyone else slows down and stares.

A Social Ref needs to be a part of every play—all the way through to the end—and often after the actual play is finished, because of game control issues like trash-talking and taunting.

It's a level of attention and engagement that the Beginner Brain isn't ready for. It doesn't follow plays through to the end and assumes plays will go a certain way. This Beginner Brain instinct tends to show up more in blow-outs: refs take plays off because the score is no longer close, and simple situations turn into big problems.

Some of the closest, *goofiest* plays occur when a player doesn't take the easy play you ASSUME they will take, and instead makes the untraditional play.

The second baseman just needs to move five steps and step on second for the third out of the inning. Instead they make a wild throw to third base, or a three-hopper to 1st for a play that is so close, it could get called either way: a **"Coin-Flip" Call**. There you are, standing flat-footed at home plate because you were about to casually announce the end of the inning, when you needed to be making a "bang bang" Coin-Flip Call at 1st base.

I once watched a defensive player in football intercept a ball with nobody within 15 yards. All he had to do was jog the ball back for an easy pick-6 touchdown. Instead he slowed down as he got to the goal line, started dancing (poorly), and kicked the ball out of his own hands, out of bounds. Did he score? Did the ball go out before the goal line? I had no idea, because I was standing on the other end of the field watching the play like a spectator, assuming no one would ever catch him.

I didn't finish the play because my Beginner Brain assumed what was easy was guaranteed. Don't "**assume easy**" in rec sports—you will constantly be surprised.

Players and fans take plays off. They stop and watch. You need to train your brain to engage on every play and move with the play until it's done.

Which brings us to our third training switch:

**DECISION SWITCH**

Stop & Think | Move To Decide

Do you remember the color of your first bike? (Mine was red with yellow padding and pedals.)

It's not really that important; what is important is what your body did when you tried to recall the image just now.

If you are like most people, you paused, tilted your head slightly back and pointed your eyes up and off to the side.

This is a classic "stop and think" pose: your body gets still and your eyes look up as your brain goes to work trying to recall or calculate something. It's a natural human instinct.

**This is bad for refs.**

You need to flip the switch to movement, and train your brain to decide on the fly.

**KEY CONCEPT**

**You need to trigger decisions with your feet first.**

In every case where you need to make a decision, move towards the decision you have to make.

**STOP & SQUASH**

Move towards your decisions, but DON'T pause and just move your HEAD. This is the **"look around"** bug. Your Beginner Brain will tell you to look around and *away* from the call, because it is instinctively looking for help that often won't be there. The best help comes from movement towards the call.

If you stop and think, or look around, you will freeze. No new ref thinks it will ever happen, until it eventually happens to them.

I had reffed football for years before I started with softball. One of my very first games there was a close play at first base . . . and I froze.

With everyone staring, I made the call as quiet and small as possible, then turned my back and faded away. Instead of upsetting one team with a lousy call, I confused both teams by trying to hide.

There is one sure way to help avoid the freeze: move. Move first, then think while you are moving. Move your feet and your brain will follow.

**Move into a call in order to make a better call.**

You will notice an interesting cue with great Social Refs: **they make a lot of one-legged "flamingo" calls**.

When you begin to move into calls and focus on the Third Game (top arrow) your feet will start to help you even more by leaning into the call with one foot up in the air like a flamingo (bottom arrow).

Standing on one leg will not make you a better umpire, but when you begin to engage with the Third Game, and flip the switches to move into Ref Brain mode, your brain begins to work with you, and not against you. It will start to do all kinds of little things you may never notice, like have you standing on one leg when you make a great call.

New refs think good decisions lead to better engagement with the game and better connections with the players. **The reverse is true: the better your engagement with the game, the better your decisions will be.**

REVERSAL

You need to move into the action, in order to trigger better decisions about the action.

**KEY CONCEPT**

**When you first start, you won't need more knowledge, you will need more movement.**

Move to think. Move to engage.

The first time I ever reffed youth basketball, I was in jeans and boots; they literally pulled me out of the stands and gave me a whistle. You'd be surprised how many careers get started this way.

The first foul I saw, I just pointed at the kid and said, "NO NO NO" over and over again, scaring the crap out of her. Maybe that's what the whistle was for.

I knew it was a foul, but I didn't know how to move my body, and use a system, in order to call the foul. You will feel when something is wrong. Turn on your Ref Brain to help you move and decide, and signal that something is wrong.

There are more components to engagement that we will discuss, but for now realize that the three training switches of the **Spectator Switch** (how you see the game), the **Connection Switch** (how you follow each play), and the **Decision Switch** (how you make decisions on your feet) all deal with your level of engagement with the game in order to make better decisions.

We bring them up now, when you're probably getting that new rule book, because most new refs get hyper-focused on seeing and reading the rules. First focus on seeing the Third Game, which is only possible by changing old instincts of how you watch, connect, and engage with the game.

**BOOK COVER**

## *Book Cover Break: Move With the Third Game*

Your ref **Book Cover** is how players judge you and your actions before you even say a word or make a call. The Book Cover is a combination of your uniform, body language, face cues, signals, and movement.

The more you can keep your hips and shoulders pointed at your decision, the easier it will be to move into the call AND visually show players you are focused on the game.

Beginning refs are not used to walking or running *backwards*, and side-stepping along sidelines.

They waste a lot of motion by always running and turning, which often gets their back turned to the action, and means they don't get their shoulders squared. Social Refs **pivot their hips often** (the Hip-Flip) so they are always facing the action, even if they are walking or running backwards, away from the action.

**PRACTICE**

Practice walking and even trying to sprint backwards before your first few shifts. New refs race back to the "right spot" on position diagrams, and miss important action. A Social Ref doesn't mind being a little out of position and walking backwards, because the whole play is in front of them.

Your Beginner Brain tries to fool you into thinking that there is a "perfect spot" on the field for positioning, and if you just hurry there, then everything will be okay. There is never a "perfect spot." It is better to have your Ref Brain **build the instinct that something is wrong anytime your back is turned.**

It's hard to see the Third Game when you are looking in the other direction.

When a play is in motion and you are hugging a sideline or foul line, side-step (or skip) along the line instead of trying to run north-and-south alongside the play.

STOP & SQUASH

When you get caught running to a better position, you often end up looking and making calls "over your shoulder," which makes decisions harder.

"Square yourself off" and face the play to improve your credibility and book cover by walking, and even running, backwards.

# Your Rule Book Sucks. . .

When ref candidates interview with Underdog, we ask what they think makes a good ref.

The top answer is always some version of: *"They need to know the rules!"*

REF MYTH

**Ref Myth**: The rule book is my friend, my safety net, my life jacket. The better I memorize it, the better I will ref.

**Ref Truth**: Your rule book sucks.

I have gotten into trouble in the past with this statement, so let's clarify a couple of things:

Your rule book is important. It's the starting point for your job. You should read it over SEVERAL times. Stop and read it right now, standing up, if you can.

. . . It still sucks, for many reasons.

It's probably really old—some Microsoft Word doc or PDF that was written at least 10 or 15 years ago.

It's too big, and too long. It has no visuals.

It lists equipment and rules and codes of conduct, but it never really tells you what's most important.

> *What are the five rules that people get wrong over and over again?*
>
> *What are the four penalties that you will call EVERY game?*
>
> *Which calls are **auto-arguments**?*
>
> *How often might you might call one penalty vs. another?*

Your rule book probably **has no priorities**. Every single rule demands your attention.

Most of all, it's missing your responses and communication.

It tries so hard to explain every factor that goes into a correct decision, but it never tells you *how to communicate your decision*.

It never teaches you how to deal with someone who really hates your decision. It never talks about what to do when everyone is confused about a correct decision.

You can read the rules all day long, but as Bruce Lee says in *Enter the Dragon*: "Boards don't hit back." Your rule book will never talk back. Every player WILL talk back, with real questions, and often with CAP.

Despite all this, new refs tend to fall in love with the rule book. It becomes the most important idea to grab on to when getting started.

Had a tough game? *Go read the rules.*

Players don't like your calls? *Tell them to go read the rules.*

Feel like you are struggling as a new ref? **Well, are you sure you know the rules?**

 **You need to learn and know the rules. Then you need to move past the rule book.**

**KEY CONCEPT**

The rule book is a bunch of vocab words and colors and nouns in a foreign language you are trying to learn.

You can cram your Beginner Brain full of new vocabulary words and repeat them well enough to pass a high school French test, but it doesn't mean you can speak the language.

Social Refs know how to speak the language of reffing.

They start with the rules, but they don't get stuck on the rules.

Rule books teach the ingredients to make decisions, like a cookbook for officials. Memorizing recipes won't make you a chef, and memorizing the rule book won't make you a ref.

# . . . And Nobody Reads It Anyway.

Another issue with the rule book: very few people read or understand it.

I don't blame people, though; I've heard the thing sucks.

**Ref Myth**: Most players know the rules. The captains and coaches *definitely* read and know the rules.

**REF MYTH**

**Ref Truth**: If 10% of your league has read the rule book, you are lucky.

Even then, "reading the rules" for a player might mean, *"I skimmed them real quick on my way to the field."*

People play in your league to have fun, not to read rules and instructions.

One of the worst things you can do, then, is ref like someone who assumes everyone reads the rules, and get really pissed off when you find out nobody has.

Farnam Street Blog (**fs.blog**), one of the best things on the internet, is where I first learned about an idea called "Hanlon's Razor":

**KEY IDEA**

**"Never attribute to malice that which can be adequately explained by neglect."**

Ever spend all night doubting yourself because your friend didn't get back to you about potential plans?

> *Was it something I said? Are they a jerk? Are they mad at me? Did I do something wrong?*

The real reason is rarely ever so dramatic. Often it's *"Aww crap. Sorry, my phone died,"* or *"I just got caught up last night."*

How silly did you feel, imagining all the worst-case scenarios and things YOU must have done wrong, when your friend just lost their phone charger?

Now think of Hanlon's Razor back on the field in a CAP situation: Are people upset with you because they truly dislike you and don't respect you (malice), or is it because no one reads your rulebook (neglect)?

No one knows the rules. . . or they know parts of the rules, and have confused your rules with another league's rules, *and* a game they watched on television the day before. The weirder the rule, the more angry and confused they will get (*like a crazy chess rule*).

A ref might know every rule in the book, but struggle to communicate the rules to people who haven't read them.

New refs use phrases that create more problems:

> *"That's not what the rule book says."*

> *"The rules clearly state. . ."*

or even worse:

*"You need to stop arguing and go read the rulebook!"*

They won't read the rules, just like you won't read the fine print on that user agreement for the new version of iTunes.

New refs also have trouble remembering what it was like when they didn't know the rules. In their great book, *Made to Stick*, Chip and Dan Heath call this concept, the "**Curse of Knowledge**."

**KEY IDEA**

**You can't remember what it was like before you learned the rule book, so you explain rules and decisions like you are talking to yourself in the present.**

You use fancy terms like "illegal contact" and "intentional grounding" and "ineligible receiver." You use abbreviations and ref jargon and concepts that people don't understand because they haven't read or studied them like you have. . . which just gets players and coaches more confused and upset.

Then *you* get more angry and take it personally, because people are questioning you when they clearly don't know the rules. . . which leads to more conflict, more confusion, more CAP.

Sometimes confused players will even demand that YOU go read the rule book.

Once in a while, that is definitely the case. You will probably remember rules incorrectly a few times. More often, players are taking bits and pieces of various rules and making up their own rule book in their head.

Rookie refs literally go on the field with a crumpled-up rule book in their pocket. They spend all day waiting for players to "break the rules" so they can lecture them:

*That's illegal. That's an infraction.* ***You can't do that; you should know better.***

The more you talk about rules and the rule book, the more your game will revolve around rules questions and confusion.

Veteran Social Refs rarely mention the rule book. They internalize the rules, and then try to **teach** them at the right times:

> *"So the way I understand the rule. . ."*
>
> *"For this league, we normally. . . "*
>
> *"It's my understanding that a player can't. . . "*

Part of climbing down off the pedestal is avoiding throwing the rule book in someone's face. It might seem like someone is attacking you personally, when really they just don't understand the rule or your explanation.

When I was in full freak-out mode over the pawn chess move, instead of showing me books and certificates, imagine if Coach Coats had said something like:

> *"Yeah, I know. It's a crazy move right? It took me years to learn it! How about this: I won't use it right now, but going forward know that it's a real move in the game. I can show you how it works later if you are interested in trying it yourself. It could help."*

Would I have kept playing (and losing at) chess with Coach for the rest of the summer? Hell yes!

Social Refs understand that true teaching is never just explaining why someone is wrong. Its having the empathy to remember that there was a time you also didn't know a confusing rule. Just because you know it now, doesn't make you special, unless you can HELP others understand it too.

Telling someone they broke a rule might create Conflict. Telling someone they broke a rule that you know and they don't will always create CAP!

Talk about the rules carefully, knowing that many people will never read them.

# Make a Ref Journal

Your rule book stinks, it doesn't teach you how to communicate, and no one reads it anyway.

Now what do we do?

Be proactive. Let's make a **Ref Journal**: a new resource that takes the rule book, skims off the best parts, and prioritizes key rules and communication sequences.

## The Ref-Journal

| Spec Section | Key Rules / Penalties |
|---|---|
| 1.<br>2.<br>3.<br>4.<br>5. | 1.<br>2.<br>3.<br>4. |
| **Key Questions / Comments**<br>1.<br>2.<br>3.<br>4. | **Script-Sheet**<br>1.<br>2.<br>3.<br>4. |

Your Ref Journal includes:

1. **League Specs Section**
2. **Key Rules/Penalties**
3. **Key Questions/Key Comments**
4. **Your Script-Sheet**

This Ref Journal exercise is helpful anytime you start with a new rule book. Last year I volunteered with the Special Olympics State Games as a Flag Football ref, so let's use their rules as an example.

First, get the rulebook and read it all the way through one time, standing up, please. We need to start learning to process rules *on our feet*.

Then grab a sheet of paper and split it into 4 quadrants. (Our Ref Journal will just be one sheet of paper to start, but will grow with more info over time.)

In the first quadrant, write down what you think are the main "Spec's" of the league–basic operational info like:

> *How many players on the field?*
> *How much time per period? Per half? Per game?*
> *How much are scores worth?*
> *How many timeouts does each team get?*

So for quadrant 1, **League Specs**, I write down:

> *5 player max/4 minimum*
> *Non-Contact League*
> *1 First Down per possession/Starts at 5-yard line*
> *1 Timeout per half*
> *Two 15-minute halves/Running clock both halves*

For quadrant 2, the **Key Rules** section, I am looking for ideas that the rule book highlights or repeats over and over again—key concepts and protocols.

So I write down:

> *1 foot in-bounds for catch*
> *7-yard Rush Line*
> *No Fumbles/ INTS dead where they are caught*
> *No Dives or Spins*
> *QB can't rush*
>
> *Knee or hand is down*
> *5 yards for 1 / 12 yards for 2*
> *5 yard No Rush zone before First Down cone and goal line*

I also look for key calls/penalties/fouls specific to the league.

In this case the rules are really simple. Every offensive penalty is minus 10 yards and a loss of down. Every defensive penalty is plus 10 yards and a first down. It seems like the penalties of rushing early and flag guarding are mentioned over and over again, so I write those two down as well.

Quadrant 3 is **Key Comments/Questions**, or as I call it, my *"have to"* section. These are key questions I feel I am going to *have to* know and answer over and over again because of normal confusion in the game. There should also be key comments to tell people without waiting for questions–things like reminders, warnings, and equipment comments. What are the five most common questions I will be asked, and what are the five common statements to proactively announce to players?

In a sense, I am learning the rule book by teaching it to myself.

I write down:

> *1 Timeout*
> *No Stopped Clock*
> *No QB Runs*
> *No Rush Zones*
> *No hands/flag guards*
> *Play is over if flags fall off*

I guess that because of these unique "Rush Zones" I will be asked *"Ref, can we run?"* quite often (turns out this was the number one question asked at the tournament).

So I simply start announcing whether it is a Run and Pass or Pass Only Zone **before each play starts**.

(Put a pin in that thought for Key Habit #3 coming up.)

I should also feel comfortable making my 'key statements' to players any time I'm on the field. Things like *"please tuck your shirt in, Green,"* or *"fix your flags,"* or *"make sure you are behind the 7-yard rush zone"* are all proactive statements that I want in my journal to try out once I get to the field.

In about 20 minutes, I have turned a 19-page rule book into one page of notes that is the foundation of a **new Ref Journal**.

Quadrant 4 is the most fun part. Your **Script-Sheet** is a key part of your Ref Journal and your communication system. It is how you will respond to situations you know are going to come up.

Someone says you missed an easy call . . . what's your response?

Here is the WORST response you can give:

>    *"No, I didn't!"*

New refs want to focus on obscure rules and fancy signals. You will make the most progress practicing your RESPONSES to situations that will come up in every sport. Worry *more* about your *response* when someone says you missed a goal-tend, instead of what the signal is for a goal-tend.

We know about CAP. We *know* no one reads your rules. So we know people are going to say certain things in certain situations—why not write down and practice your responses?

 How do you think comedians and performers handle hecklers on the big stage? **They practice their responses ahead of time.** They learn to expect hecklers, and they

PRACTICE    learn how to deal with them. Practicing and role-playing scripted responses can help you avoid making snap reactions to predictable situations and saying what feels good in the moment . . . exactly how the Beginner Brain villain hopes you communicate.

**SCRIPT SHEET**

**Start your Script-Sheet (Questions 1-3):** How do you respond to the following CAP situations? Can you write down your responses and practice out loud in front of the mirror?

*"Oh man, that's the worst call I have ever seen."*

*"Why didn't you make that call? Everyone saw it!"*

*"Are you sure about that rule, ref?"*

We will keep adding questions as we move along through new phases. Just know that *this* is a big missing piece to every rule book: scripting your communication, and practicing common responses.

Your rule book may suck, but you don't. Teach yourself the rules by building a Ref Journal. Write down your basic scripts. Work with a friend on them. It may feel a little corny, but it will make you better, and prepare your Ref Brain for the situations you know are going to come up in any game.

# The "Hidden" Jobs

Most training programs miss a basic idea:

**KEY CONCEPT**

**Social Refs don't have one job; they have FIVE.**

The jobs are always there, but most are hidden in the Learning Phase, and never mentioned in that rule book. Becoming a great Social Ref often depends on learning and managing these additional hidden jobs.

# 5 JOBS OF A SOCIAL REF

15% **TEACHER & COACH**

25% **REF & UMP**

30% **ANNOUNCER & SCORE BOARD**

20% **FIELD & GEAR MANAGER**

10% **LEAGUE OPERATIONS**

**Ref and Ump:** *You* make decisions and calls based on the rules and seeing the Third Game.

**Teaching and Coaching:** *You* help people learn the rules and avoid common mistakes, especially with new players and subs. Sometimes a reminder or warning can result in fewer calls that need to be made.

**Announcer and Scoreboard:** Game info is the start of your engagement and credibility because *you* control the scoreboard. With more experience, you can work on your "Announcer's Voice" to more easily communicate with players.

**Field and Gear Manager:** *You* need to own the field and keep track of all the gear the players may use, especially if your league is providing equipment.

**League Operations:** Admin tasks like rosters, shirts, waivers, announcements, payments, pictures, and prizes may end up falling on *you*, determining who can play in your game and how fast your game starts.

You may not think Social Reffing stacks up with the Pro's, but in some cases the Pros have it easier! There are about 7 refs on an NFL football field, you probably have two. In an MLB Baseball game there are normally four umpires. In rec softball, kickball, and even little league baseball (a grouping we'll call, "The Trio") there is normally just one home plate umpire.

The Pros may get yelled at more, and the games may move much faster, but they don't have to worry about announcing basic scoreboard info, teaching simple rules, and checking to see if someone walks on the field wearing sandals! Keep these ideas in mind as we move into Phase 3 and hit the field for your first shift. It's easier to see the Third Game when you understand the additional jobs you may have as a Social Ref.

## PHASE 2 RECAP

The learning and training phase asks you to look beyond the obvious stuff—rules, handbooks, and tests—to see what many new refs miss when they start out.

**KEY IDEAS**

- Watching sports on TV teaches your brain and eyes bad habits (TV Ball).

- Every game has multiple games within it depending on your perspective. Learn to see the Third Game as a ref (Spectator Switch), and to engage with it at all times (Connection Switch).

- "Look off-ball"–focusing on the **feet** first–to better see the Third Game.

- Once you connect with the Third Game, don't be surprised when you see situations and actions that no one else will notice (Neo Principle).

- Your rule book stinks, and no one reads it. Don't take it personally, and don't get stuck on it; create your own Ref Journal focusing on game specs, important rules and penalties, key questions and comments, and your scripted responses in your Script-Sheet.

- One of your hidden jobs is to teach the rules to players while remembering the "Curse of Knowledge".

- A Social Ref normally has at least *five* jobs. Reffing and Umping is just **one** of them.

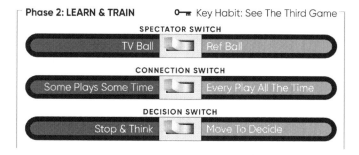

SPECTATOR SWITCH

TV Ball | Ref Ball

CONNECTION SWITCH

Some Plays Some Time | Every Play All The Time

DECISION SWITCH

Stop & Think | Move To Decide

## PRACTICE

Attend a live game and practice "looking off-ball", watching the opposite of what other the fans focus on.

Take your rulebook and start building a Ref Journal with the 4 main sections, including your Script-Sheet.

Read and practice scripts standing up. Practice moving into calls with your feet before you decide on them.

Practice walking and even running backwards while keeping your shoulders squared.

**BOOK COVER**

## *Book Cover Break: Preparing to Hit the Field*
## *Jay's First Shift*

Your first few games are going to be a blur. You may feel uncertain, and your brain will want to hide because you are so new to the rules and the league. Here are some memories from the legend Jay about his first shift:

"My first shift as a flag football ref fell on a chilly November night. Even though I'd seen the reffing uniform a million times watching sports, *I now felt like a fraud actually putting it on*. When you wear stripes you immediately feel, "I should know the rules better than anyone," but that was not the case. The uniform screams "come ask me" about rules or reasoning behind my call. It would be great if I could respond with "That's a great question—I have no idea, bud," but that wouldn't fly."

Even with my office training, I feared being stationary and making it easier for players to approach me. So I hustled like no other.

 **I didn't know the rules well, so I decided to hide behind hustle.**

**KEY IDEA**

You can't get mad at a guy who is flying all over the place and sweating in 40 degree weather! The veteran ref I was working with said I was "over-hustling" and it felt like I burned about 50,000 calories. I sprinted to every spot, I ran to the middle of the field, I over-shared the Down and I perfected the back pedal.

I wasn't going to give a player the opportunity to say, *"Ohhh, you're a NEW ref."* I tried to give the impression that "this guy is constantly moving and totally engaged" and I tried to look like I belonged.

Most new refs have those moments where they do everything right and ask, *"Why am I getting yelled at?"* I followed steps 1, 2 and 3 and everyone is angry at me. They start to wonder, *"Do I benefit from not making that call going forward?"* Some of the best advice I gave to other new refs working through that first scary shift is just telling them, *"You did everything right, that player just had to get it out. You probably saved a dog from getting kicked ."* Don't hide from doing the right thing even when you're new. If you need to hide, then try hiding behind your signals and your hustle.

## PHASE 3: SURVIVE (FIRST 15 GAMES)

# KEY HABIT: BECOME THE SCOREBOARD

You decided why you wanted to ref in Phase 1. You started learning and training in Phase 2. Now it's time to get going. We need to make some growth rep mistakes and survive the first 15 games. It's going to be confusing and tough, but we have already flipped some switches and have some tools to practice, including our Ref Journal. (You stopped and ran through the Ref Journal exercise, right?)

Your first shift will be scary . . . don't worry. It was scary for everyone, no matter your training.

After CAP, the second most common reason new refs fail is because they miss the hidden scoreboard and announcer job. Nobody believes their calls or decisions, because their game info is always wrong.

"Becoming the scoreboard" with your game info starts the **Engagement Circle**. It forms the basis of your Core Communication Sequence (CCS).

You will want to hit the field and make big calls to show you belong. All of your decisions will become easier once you start the third **Key Habit** of providing simple game info and becoming the scoreboard.

## Joe's Second Shift

Eastlake Playfield, Seattle, WA—June 2018

*"Nobody here believes that call except for you!"*

That's the captain's reaction to a close call at second base by Joe the Ump.

Even though Joe has reffed over a hundred flag football games, on this sunny summer day he is working his second ever kickball shift as a home plate ump, square in the Survival Phase.

The play is close, but Joe's call is 100% correct; he had great position right near the base. . . but Joe is also new to kickball so he makes a very common Survival Phase mistake:

He makes the call quick and quiet—basically to himself—and "fades away" from it fast.

*"Got 'em,"* he mutters under his breath, keeping his hand next to his waist as he flashes a quick "out" signal before turning and walking away.

Neither team understands or even hears the call. The runner at Second shrugs her shoulders, confused: *"Am I safe or out?"*

No wonder the captain uses the word *"believes"*—Joe calls it small, like he doesn't even believe it.

The captain is first confused as to what the call is, then mad once he realizes the call is "OUT at second".

He starts arguing with Joe; soon everyone else on the team joins in. So Joe makes the second common survival mistake: he tries to respond to every single question and comment about his call in real time. He gets defensive and pleads his case: the runner hadn't gotten to the bag yet, and he made the best call he could.

The conversation is heated but doesn't get out of hand, and the game eventually starts to move on to the next play.

This is actually Joe's worst moment of the game. . . Can you guess why?

Hyper-focused on defending his call—trying to answer every question and complaint—he forgets to that two runs scored on the play. The game is now 8-6 instead of 6-6.

A player points out that the score is wrong, so Joe goes and flips the scoreboard to read 7-6. Then another player reminds him that two runs scored. Joe stops, thinks through the play in front of both teams, then goes back AGAIN to flip the scoreboard to read 8-6.

Joe will now have a tough time on every big play and close call, no matter the situation, because of a humbling moment when **he lost track of the game info**.

When getting started, don't forget the most basic responsibility of a Social Ref:

**No matter the calls, big or small, good or bad, YOU are the scoreboard.**

Joe is an *amazing* ref—one of the best I have ever watched. I've never seen him make an incorrect call in 3 years! But you have to be bigger and better than just being right to be a great referee. **You have to "become the scoreboard" for players to trust and believe in your calls.**

On that Tuesday afternoon, Joe actually made the three most common survival mistakes on one play, even while making the "correct" call.

Joe (and many new refs):

> **Reverse when they should "ref big" and "ref small."**
>
> **Start off as "Squirrels" and fall into the "Customer Service Trap."**
>
> **Lose track of game info and miss the hidden scoreboard job.**

This is a **Volcano Call**: a play where the ump technically makes the correct call, but the way the call is made causes players, fans, captains and coaches to blow their top, and results in lots of unnecessary CAP.

People tend to think they are very unique. When it comes to player instincts and reactions, they are actually quite similar.

One weekend I reffed flag football in Seattle on a Saturday afternoon and called an easy and obvious pass interference. *"I was just going for the ball, ref!"* the player yelled back at me.

The next day, I drove two hundred miles and reffed flag football in Portland, Oregon, where an almost identical pass interference happened. You'll never guess what the player yelled at me:

*"Ref, I was just going for the ball!"*

Many players in your league are actually the same. No one reads the rules, very few people will like or believe your calls, and nobody is ever guilty of a penalty or foul. The only people that admit they are guilty are Red from *The Shawshank Redemption*, and one guy 9 years ago who said, *"That's a really good call on me for PI."* Players in different sports and different leagues will act—and react—very similarly to calls they don't understand and don't like.

New refs all act the same, too. We have seen that call from Joe a thousand times.

New refs default to watching the game from one spot—shoulders hunched over and feet stuck in cement, clutching a whistle or stopwatch or clicker as tightly as possible. They scan the field, looking for a "hero call" to make—to "show" they are a ref—and forget to answer the fundamental question on everyone's mind:

*What does the scoreboard say?*

When I first trained in as a Softball ump, for some reason it was really important in my Beginner Brain to watch for players missing a base when rounding second or third—a classic example of the **Over-Ref Switch**. Meanwhile, I missed the obvious stuff—my games would break down and get stuck in arguments about whether there were actually one or two outs recorded in the inning.

You can stand out from all the other mediocre refs by doing something really simple:

**Build the core habit of giving out game info and "become the scoreboard."**

Great Social Refs master this core habit first. They practice to make game info *automatic*, because it's the habit to unlocking everything else that you need to do as a ref, and it's the number one factor to surviving your first 15 games. Quality decisions, game control, movement and hustle, and working the 5 jobs all connect back to your engagement as a ref. And your engagement STARTS with game info.

# THE ENGAGEMENT CIRCLE

Game info isn't a bonus, or an add-on, *it is the game*. New refs treat it like a chore; they want to start with calls and rulings (the end of the circle), and only give out game info when asked. If your game info is always a reaction—and you need to stop and think and calculate it every time you are asked—then every other engagement idea will suffer.

Your Beginner Brain asks all kind of questions when you first ref:

> *Was that a penalty?*
>
> *Why is this guy yelling at me and acting so crazy?*
>
> *Did I do something wrong?*
>
> *Was that the right call?*
>
> *How do they expect me to see that?*

The Ref Brain is focused on the most important questions:

**KEY CONCEPT**

*What does the scoreboard say? What game info do the players need right now, even if they haven't asked?*

Your signals, your calls, your movement, and your communication—everything starts with your game info. You will be more involved in your game—*and* become more credible—when you are constantly asking yourself about the crucial game info and providing it to your players by becoming the scoreboard.

# The Cell Phone Photographer

You're walking down the street and a family on vacation asks you to take their picture with one of their cell phones. You smile, taking the photos and giving a common response:

> *"I took a bunch of pictures, so hopefully one of them turns out good."*

We take a "bunch of pictures" because digital photography makes this easy, and because everyone has been bummed out when the only picture features one person with their eyes closed, another making a weird face, and another looking away.

We take five pictures because taking *only one* minimizes our chance of success.

We take five pictures because *one* will actually work.

Once you understand your first and most important responsibility is to become the scoreboard and give out game info, your next question is:

> *How often do I do that?*

The answer is: **as much as possible**. Maybe even three, four, or five times a play. . . just like you would take digital photos on a cellphone.

Most new refs start with a bad habit of **One-and-Done Communication**: they announce a sequence or a piece of game info only once before moving along. . . then they get frustrated fifteen seconds later when someone asks them for that very same info.

*"Didn't you hear me the first time?"* they think, and sometimes even *say* out loud (an auto-escalator)!

No, the player did NOT hear you.

They were talking to their teammate, getting ready for the next play— just generally focused on something else—and it went right over their head. These are the people blinking or looking away when you take just one photo.

Taking only one cell phone photo is lame, because it's so easy to take five. Practicing One-and-Done Communication is worse, because you're building lazy habits for your system. The Beginner Brain always tricks you into thinking one is good enough.

Engagement starts with your game info, and depends on your frequency.

Consider two things:

 **It is really hard to be too loud in a rec league game.**

KEY CONCEPT

The pro's have speakers and announcers. In a rec league, you are the announcer, even though you have no microphone. Almost every new ref starts too quiet, because they don't understand they are now the announcer for a huge gym, or a large field. Sound just disappears. In 18 years, I have NEVER once had a ref or ump start by being too loud.

Be loud without seeming like you are barking orders at people. You will find the sweet spot over time.

**KEY CONCEPT**

**It is almost impossible to repeat the core game info too many times.**

FREQUENCY SWITCH

1 And Done | 3-Rep Communication

Want to instantly become a better ref?

**When you give game info, repeat it 3 times.**

We call this a **3-Rep Habit**.

A "One-and-Done" ref is trying to get the game info out of the way, like crossing something off a To-do list. Announcing the scoreboard is for the game, for the players, and ALSO for YOU.

You say the core game info at least three times—like photos on a cellphone—so one of them works.

You don't need to say it 3 times in a row like a robot, but say it at least 3 times, and your whole experience as a ref will change.

**REF MYTH**

**Ref Myth:** Repeating the game info is boring. Everybody already knows it.

**Ref Truth:** Repetition builds trust.

The first batter of the game hits a pop fly to the second baseman. That's one out on your scoreboard.

> *"Catch is good for one out,"* you yell.

> *"Time called, one away,"* you say next.

After walking back to home plate, you turn to the batter and say:

> *"Batter, I have one down for you."*

Then you show one finger to the pitcher and say, *"One out"* as you get back in your stance.

You have just given the out four different times in four different ways. That may feel like a lot, and it may feel unnecessary, but guess what?

Now you will seldom have arguments about outs, avoiding that CAP altogether, saving your energy and credibility for big **Coin-Flip Calls** at first base.

New refs can't separate CAP that's built into the job—coin-flip calls and auto-arguments—from CAP that crops up because of confusion (reffing small) and bad info habits. Prevent confusion CAP and game info arguments by building a 3-Rep Habit.

Games don't really spin out of control because of "bad calls"—they turn into raging dumpster fires because *no one trusts the calls.* You lose your credibility when you lose track of the game info: people don't believe you can handle the big tricky stuff, because you couldn't handle the small basic stuff.

In one of my first few kickball games—in survival mode just like Joe—I started my own dumpster fire: as teams walked off the field after the third out of the inning, I scolded them and called them back, saying, *"What's wrong with you guys? There are only two outs!"*

Both teams pointed out that there were actually three outs. How do you think the rest of that game went for me, with my credibility blown?

More importantly, how did I respond? How will you respond the first time it happens in your game?

Will you get mad at the players? Will you fight back and demand that they listen and trust you more? Will you give up and say, *"Reffing is not for me"*? Or will you take a look at your system, starting with how you handle your info habits?

**Ref Myth:** The best refs are great because they rarely make mistakes.

**Ref Truth:** Social Refs make *a lot* of mistakes—more than those who flame-out in their first fifteen games—but those mistakes are growth reps that make their info habits and system better.

When you build the habit of game info, players begin trusting you, and asking you questions they don't ask other refs.

When you create a strong scoreboard, and a player questions the game info, another player on their own team will correct them.

When you build up credibility with constant communication, you will catch your own info mistakes faster, before they lead to meltdowns—like giving out a fifth down.

Up your frequency with the 3-Rep Habit, and become the scoreboard to start earning trust with players.

# Your Core Communication Sequence (CCS)

Some game info is more valuable than others. We want to feed players game info that has a **high priority**.

Think back to the main engagement question: *What will players ask me over and over again, sometimes every play?*

**KEY CONCEPT**

**Most sports have at least one sequence that is the core priority for every play: the Core Communication Sequence or CCS.**

Game info can get very big and very broad: the score, game time, whether the clock is running, timeouts, fouls, and much more. In survival mode, we want to identify the one or two communication sequences you will use the most, that can be announced before every play or key action, with the 3-Rep Habit.

For flag football, the CCS is normally easy: you have a down and distance before every play starts. Some co-rec leagues have an additional gender component.

When we train refs for Underdog Flag Football, our CCS is **DDG**:

**Down/Distance/Gender** for every co-ed play, and **Down/Distance** for every Gentlemen's League play.

Our *priority* is to announce and show the down and distance on every single play because that is the question we will get the most.

You could probably get away with skipping the CCS for a few plays without announcing it—I have certainly watched hundreds of refs try—because *"nobody asked them for it."*

**Don't skip it. This will come back to bite you every time.**

In "The Trio" of kickball, softball, and baseball, our CCS takes one of two tracks based on how the play began.

If a ball is put in play (fair territory), we like to use **ThOR**:

> **Time/hands/Outs/Runs** <the "h" is small for the ACTION of raising your hands up—you don't say "hands" out loud!>
>
> *Time Called!* <hands straight up> *One down, and one across on the play!*

If a ball is not put in play (fouled off or just a pitch taken) we use **LoBS**:

> **Location/Balls/Strikes**
>
> *Inside* for *Ball 2, brings up 2-O on the count!*

Sports like basketball or soccer may not have a clear cut "every play" CCS, but both sports are similar in their signals and their spoken communication when it comes to out of bounds plays, changes of possession, and fouls (foul shots or penalty kicks).

Even when I ref 7-year-old basketball at the community center, I repeat some version of **Whistle/Team Color/Direction** over and over again.

> *<Whistle>*. **Red Ball** *going* **this way**.

In the higher ranks, my basketball friend Will uses:

> **<Whistle> Color/Number/Consequence (Action)**

> **<Whistle>** Red/15/Foul on the Arm/2 shots

When we evaluate flag football, kickball, or softball candidates for Underdog, we don't let you go out to the field unless you can tell us the CCS during your audition in the classroom. You don't even get to *start* survival mode until you can correctly explain the CCS during a mock game.

Bruce Lee has a saying we refer to often:

**KEY IDEA**

**"I fear not the man who has practiced ten thousand kicks once, but I fear the man who has practiced one kick ten thousand times."**

Your rule book can feel like it has ten thousand kicks when you first get started. It might not mention a CCS, but you will figure out one fast, if you pay attention.

Your CCS is the one kick you will use ten thousand times. It unlocks all the other kicks you can use, and more importantly unlocks the confidence to use them. I have spoken and consulted with all kinds of rec leagues across the country; the answers to many of their questions and problems always seems to start with the CCS, **because it can *literally* start every play**.

Great Social Refs master the "one kick" of their CCS first, and that frees up their mind to work on other questions and problems.

Our DDG Core Communication Sequence for flag football came from one ref on a normal Sunday who had their Ref Brain deliver a better way to track info. Everyone else immediately started copying **Down/ Distance/Gender** because it was a better sequence. Fifteen years later, it's the foundation of our entire training system.

Your CCS is an opportunity—it can be glue that connects you to players. They will learn to look to you for info that they want and need.

You can tell when your game info is clicking, because players will begin "**echoing**" back what you announce.

> *"1$^{st}$ and Goal, 2 plays open!"* you say before the play starts.

> *"1$^{st}$ down guys, let's stop them here!"* a player will echo back, re-enforcing the scoreboard.

When beginning refs skip the CCS, everything else becomes harder.

SCRIPT SHEET

**Question #4 on your Script Sheet: What is your CCS?** What are the components, what is the order, and when is the optimal time to provide it?

Does your sport have a CCS? Can you create one? If so, that's something you can practice even before you start your first game. In front of a mirror, standing up, saying it out loud for your cat or dog to hear. Find your CCS to help become the scoreboard.

# The Remember Trap

The most important skill good rec refs utilize is communication.

The most important part of that communication is your game information.

And your most important game info is your CCS—the one or two sequences you will use every play or action.

It's all fairly simple, except for a small issue: every other habit, instinct, and idea you have leftover in your Beginner Brain will try and get in the way of making your game info and CCS the foundation of your communication system.

If it was really so easy, then Underdog—and hundreds of other leagues—wouldn't struggle to find good refs every single day.

So let's talk about three big Beginner Brain switches that we need to flip in order to become the scoreboard and survive the first fifteen games.

A quick confession: I have problems with keys.

One morning I went across town and forgot my wife's car key in my pocket, sticking her with no car seat and a 2-year-old.

Another day I spent 4 hours walking around a park, looking for a lost house key, beating myself up the whole time.

In the early days, Underdog had frequent fire drills that involved an ump forgetting a key to an equipment box or a light tower, and having someone else race across town to deliver the "forgotten key".

The first time an ump forgets a key, you blame them and try to create more notes and reminders. *Don't forget the key this time!* The 50th time it happens, well, you need a better system.

*Now* my wife has a second car key I had made for her. *Now* I keep all my keys hooked to my belt loop, even though people make fun of me for looking like a janitor. And *now* we have a key box at every field that Underdog uses.

It's much easier to make more keys than beating yourself up about always "remembering" them.

**Replicating and repeating is better than "remembering."**

**KEY CONCEPT**

Maybe it ruined your day when you forgot to bring your laptop charger to work. Maybe next time you can have a laptop charger at home, *and* another one at work, and use that remembering brain power for something more valuable.

A second key, a second charger—these are **Universal Solutions**: ideas that take "remembering" out of your routines and habits to help you avoid potential problems.

When I first trained as kickball ump, I was taught to only call "time" when a play ended with runners on base. I tried to *remember* this, but sometimes there were runners on base and sometimes there weren't, so sometimes I remembered and sometimes I forgot. I didn't build the habit of calling time and triggering my CCS.

Your Beginner Brain tells you to keep things this complicated, because a "real ump" will always remember to check the runners on base.

You're umping co-ed kickball! **Call time at the end of every play!** It's a Universal Solution.

When should you remember to write down a score on your clipboard or scorebook?

How about every time someone scores!

**KEY CONCEPT**
***Remembering* is not a system; it's just something you tell yourself will work, when you don't actually have a system.**

Your system needs to be based off "triggers" that tell you to do something the same way every time. This is the idea behind Universal Habits and Solutions: *Every time X happens, do Y and say Z.*

Think back to Joe's Volcano play at second base: he could have avoided a lot of CAP later on if the end of the play had just naturally triggered his CCS of **ThOR**: Time, (hands), Outs, Runs.

> *"**Time** called—**2 outs** and **2 across** on the play."*

"2 Across" is the trigger to go flip the scoreboard, no matter how angry your players.

Instead, Joe's instinct to defend his call got in the way of announcing his CCS, and his scoreboard and his engagement suffered.

Rookie refs think they can just "remember" the scoreboard when it matters, and turn on habits when games get late or close. Spending time trying to remember will get in the way of your important decisions.

With two minutes left in a flag-football game—how often should you announce the game clock?

If the game clock is on a stopwatch, hanging around your neck, announce it every play!

When you use Universal Habits, your brain feels something you MUST do is incomplete (a powerful force) instead of trying to remember if you SHOULD or COULD do something.

If players come up to you demanding info and explanations while you are on the way to write down a score, or move a marker, or reset your stopwatch, you need to have the confidence to ask them to wait a second so they don't short-circuit your habits and literally mess up the scoreboard.

Imagine if Joe told the angry players, *"Let me get your 2 runs on the scoreboard, then you can tell me how bad that last call was."*

Young refs use their memory muscle less than ever. Nowadays, you don't have to remember how to spell (auto-correct), you never need to remember directions (plug it in your phone), and you don't need to remember the history or facts of anything (just type it into Google). They take this mentality onto the field, and don't log basic game info, because they are used to having their smart phone bail them out. When they try and just *remember* routines and game info, it seldom works.

Is success in your league—or even your life—based on remembering to do things? Are you over-complicating an announcement or info habit with too many "if/then" variables, when you should just try doing the same thing every time instead?

Look for Universal Habits and Solutions to build into your system—frequency and simplicity can help get rid of remembering.

# Habit Stress

Clickers, whistles, scorebooks, flags, Yellow Cards—new refs default to keeping their ref gear in a different spot every time.

They seem to wear different shorts or pants or jackets every day. They can't build patterns for tracking info or sequences for announcing game info because they can't find their stuff.

That's Habit Stress.

New refs battle two kinds of Habit Stress—1) *Where is your stuff?* and 2) *Where is your info?*

If you treat your ref gear like your car keys, and constantly keep things in a different spot after every play, then your ability to make instinctive calls and build habits will be slowed down before you can even get started.

Many new football refs go to throw a penalty with their brand new yellow penalty flag, except it's missing when they reach for it because they are putting it in a different spot in their pocket or their waistband every play.

Then the flag comes out really "late" . . . and they look indecisive, and unsure of the call.

Where does your system say your penalty flag belongs *at all times*, not just when you remember?

New flag football refs, basketball refs, and soccer refs struggle with blowing the whistle at the right time. A new football ref will often blow their whistle the first time they see a penalty, even if the play is still going. I have watched new basketball refs blow their whistle when a 3-pointer is made, bringing the whole game to a halt.

This happens when refs start a play with their whistle in their mouth, because they haven't built a habit for handling the whistle every play.

"Inadvertent whistles" are a very common rookie mistake, and can derail an entire game. The whistle doesn't belong in your mouth to start the play if you are in the first 15 games. It will just be too easy to form bad habits.

Take a page from Shawn Achor and his "20-Second Rule":

**KEY IDEA**

**If you struggle with a bad habit like watching too much TV, make it harder to turn the TV on by taking the batteries out of the remote and keeping them in your drawer.**

(Maybe this also helps with the TV Ball habit!)

If you have a bad habit like blowing your whistle at the wrong times, don't keep your whistle in your mouth! Give yourself the extra seconds to break the habit by keeping it in your hand.

It's hard to make your game info and CCS automatic when you can't instinctively find your whistle, or your scorebook, and when you have bad systems on how to use your stuff once it's located.

One shift, I noticed a new ref basically reffing with "one hand": signaling with only one hand, switching between his scorebook and whistle in the same hand, and even running down the field with one arm out and one arm by his waist. It was only later I realized he was using his second hand to hold up his pants because they were two sizes too big.

Forget about game info or the CCS—the core habit this poor ref was building in the FIRST SHIFT of his survival phase was remembering to hold his pants up. We quickly got him a new pair of pants, hopefully avoiding the unnecessary "stress" of having his pants fall down during a game.

**Keep things boring and consistent through good habits to create good long term results.**

You need the boring habit the most when things are the least boring. It's the close, tense game that is heading to the last inning, or the last two minutes that will make you miss your habits because you can't find your stuff.

New refs also fall into the Remember Trap with their game info, creating more stress.

Some of the info seems so simple. There are only 3 outs. Maybe there are only 2 timeouts. Some leagues have 1 timeout per half.

Our kickball league only has 2 strikes (an accelerated count) until you are out.

Surely you can remember that!

**REF MYTH**

**Ref Myth:** I don't need help remembering small numbers!

**Ref Truth:** As the day goes on, it's harder to remember even the easiest numbers.

Remembering is not a system.

Use your ref tools, like a clicker or a score book. Write it down.

If the score of your game is only 1-0, figure out a way to write it down.

Don't ditch tools that umps and refs have used for decades because you think you are special or have a great memory.

Much like a waiter who doesn't write your order down, and then ends up getting it wrong, beginning refs create avoidable stress by using poor habits with scoreboard info or game ideas they need to track. Sometimes you might need to write down injuries, questions from players, or awards like a player of the game.

If you aren't "in charge" of certain scoreboard info, write it down anyway. You are going to get asked by the players.

Crappy refs find reasons to avoid tracking info, and then they end up in crappy situations later on.

Social Refs just embrace the info, and become the scoreboard.

When in doubt, get it out of your head. Get it down on paper, in a notebook, on a clicker, or somewhere! Figure out where your ref gear and tools should live every play, and use those tools to help build Universal Habits that never rely on remembering.

# Reffing Big and Small

**REVERSAL**

Beginning refs want to make big calls, but a funny thing happens when they get out on the field: they ref BIG on the easy calls, and ref really SMALL on the close and important ones.

**Reffing small** means your signals, volume, repetition, and movement don't match the closeness or importance of the call you need to make. It confuses players and makes them doubt your decisions.

When it really matters, we want to **Ref big**.

Your Beginner Brain agrees that Reffing big is important, with one small trick. It tells you to Ref big, with big volume and signals, when the play is easy and nothing matters.

A batter swings and misses at strike three and the ump yells "STRIKE 3, BATTER IS OUT!" as loud as possible (totally unnecessary and often embarrassing for the batter).

When the next batter takes a pretty pitch on the right-hand corner of the plate for a potential third strike, the ump pauses, make a weird noise—like "*uhhhh*"—and looks around and off to the side.

When someone accidentally runs over an opposing player in soccer or basketball, and is apologizing and helping them up off the ground, saying, *"My bad!"*, the ref calls a foul loud and clear.

When a different player runs someone over and just keeps going, the ref swallows their whistle and runs right along with them.

A player drops an easy wide open pass in the End Zone—a new ref makes a huge incomplete signal and blows their whistle loudly.

When that same receiver is bobbling the ball and tapping one toe on the sideline as they fall out of bounds, the ref freezes and looks to the ref on the other side of the field for help, even though the action is right in front of THEM, and their call to make.

We know why this happens. The brain senses a "Lesson" coming on, and it doesn't want to deal with the CAP. Most new refs instinctively don't like big contact calls and close coin-flip calls. They avoid, fade away fast, and make them quick, quiet, and small—or sometimes not at all.

Most sports have these built in **auto-argument calls**—you could even call them **CAP calls**. These are calls that will get argued almost every single time:

- Pass Interference
- Penalty Kick Awarded
- Block or Charge Under the Basket when both players fall down
- Play at First, where the first baseman **bobbles** the ball or has trouble finding the bag with their foot
- Intentional Grounding*

(*If they removed the "Intentional" and just left it as "Grounding," there would probably be fewer arguments—NFL, you can thank me later.)

New refs don't have experience with auto-arguments and Coin-Flip Calls, so they ref big when it doesn't matter, and then ref really small when it matters most. Everyone notices when you ref big on the easy and obvious stuff to cover up your instinct to ref small on the close stuff.

Part of reffing big is getting outside of the signal box, with your hands and arms.

# THE SIGNAL BOX

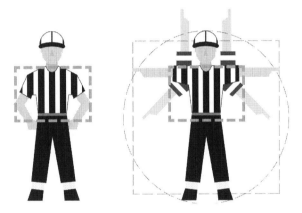

New refs watch and stare instead of signaling. Then, when pushed, they get stuck INSIDE the signal box and signal small and close to their chest because they haven't built the info habit of showing and connecting game info to their hands and arms.

Next time you are watching sports on TV, start to signal along with the plays you see. Connect the game info to your hands. Make the actual signals for "Incomplete" or "Out" with your arms and hands instead of just thinking through them in your head.

Try standing in front of the TV with the volume off, and

literally umping or reffing the game. Practice announcing the calls and **Reffing big**: being *loud* with *strong* signals OUTSIDE the signal box.

Small signals and quiet announcements to yourself make players feel like you are trying to hide the calls from them.

When you ref big, you make a Coin-Flip Call like it's the most obvious thing you have ever seen. The closer the call, the BIGGER you need to ref—with your voice or whistle volume, your movement, and your arms and hands.

A good call is a BIG call, before it's a correct call. Small, volcano calls, undermine yourself, your system, and your fellow refs.

We have found over the years that a lot of refs and umps love gambling. We used to think this was just a funny idea, that refs make extra money and hit the casino, but now I'm not so sure. Refs deal in probabilities and incomplete information, just like when you gamble.

If you only make a call, when you are 100% certain, you probably won't make very many calls the game needs.

Can you make the call when you are 80% confident? 70%? 60%?

Part of being a ref is making calls and decisions with the best info and angle you have at the time. There is no instant replay like you get on TV. You have to decide and go in the moment. You need to ref BIG, even when you are at 60%. Even when it's a coin flip, that will produce an automatic argument.

If you ref small because you're worried about possibly being wrong, you are already reffing wrong.

Don Cheadle, playing Miles Davis in the film, *Miles Ahead*, said it best:

 **"If you're gonna be wrong, BE WRONG STRONG!"**

**KEY IDEA**

Reffing small will wreck your chance to become the scoreboard, and sink players' confidence in your decisions.

**Don't worry about being wrong, worry about being heard and understood.** In the next phase, we'll learn how to deal with players who think you're wrong.

Whether the call is perfect, or wrong, make the call the RIGHT way: ref BIG to survive tough calls and close situations.

BOOK COVER

## *Book Cover Break: Protect Your Uniform*

As a ref, the players are all *watching* you.

Even when you aren't actively reffing a game, they are watching. When you pull up in your car, when you set up the field, when you're talking on your phone before the game–they are watching. When you sit down on the ground at halftime and complain to another ref about a player. . . They are *still* watching you.

Everyone is watching, and everyone is comparing. They are comparing you to every ref and ump they have ever seen, live or on TV. Don't undermine yourself by ignoring your uniform and dismissing your book cover.

There is an expectation of what a ref looks like, how a ref acts, and how a ref conducts themselves. The good news is that you can use this to your advantage. There is a power to the zebra stripes of a ref, or the sharp polo of a softball ump. An umpire's mask, a clicker, a brush, a whistle, a penalty flag—all of these items are symbols that carry power, right up to the point when you screw them up:

- · When you wear your ref hat backwards, or leave it at home and wear the ball-cap of your favorite team instead, you mess up your Book Cover.

- · When you wear goofy-colored socks, or weird-looking shoes, or a strange undershirt beneath your uniform, or royal blue gym shorts that clash with your black and white ref stripes, you mess up your Book Cover.

- When you wear your "lucky" Elvis sunglasses to the field, you mess up your book cover.

New refs want to stand out and get players' attention. Earn attention with your communication, scoreboard info, movement and hustle. Don't get people's attention with clothes and uniform choices that have a poor comparison to their expectation of a professional ref. Don't try and standout with your uniform. Stand out with your engagement and game info.

**SIMPLE START**

**Start simple: tuck your dang shirt in.** Some refs love to untuck their shirts because they think it makes them look cool and "laid-back." You never, ever see refs and umps on TV with their shirts untucked. It just doesn't happen.

People often judge with their eyes before their brain or their heart.

Tuck your dang shirt in.

New refs worry about making mistakes on a call or ruling. The first mistake they make is looking like a goofball who has no business being a ref.

*Tuck in your dang shirt!*

# The Customer Service Trap

New refs think that being liked by players means they are doing a good job. They want to give "good customer service," so they fall back on the old saying, *"The customer is always right"*. This won't work on the field. Your customers are often competing against each other in a sports game; they literally can't all be right!

We call refs who spend their first games darting around trying to fix every single thing, "Squirrels." These refs spend too much time on things that rarely matter. Squirrels focus on tiny calls, and react instantly to questions, comments, and distractions because they want everything to be perfect in the name of "customer service." They want to make EVERYONE happy.

Squirrels want to answer every question, explain every detail, fix every cone and disc perfectly, have a comeback to every comment, and they want to master all ten thousand of Bruce Lee's kicks in their first fifteen games.

Squirrels over-ref, over-explain, and most importantly, they fall right into the Customer Service Trap.

Give good customer service. Be a sympathetic teacher when no one has read the rulebook. Become the Scoreboard. Hustle your ass off and be in good position to make strong calls. But don't ref to make everyone happy, because that's impossible.

Not every question needs an answer. Not every 'issue' needs an immediate fix. Not every comment needs a response or an explanation.

Some comments may seem directed at you, but they are actually **Defender Comments**: things players say to teammates to make them feel better. . . which will feel insulting if you, the ref, decided to take them personally.

I'm umping a softball game one summer day, and the pitcher throws four consecutive balls to the WORST batter on the other team. Three of the four pitches aren't even close. After the batter walks, the shortstop turns to the pitcher and says:

>  *"Man, the ump must be using a different strike zone."*

Early on, my Beginner Brain would have produced an instant—and bad—response to that comment:

*"No sir, my strike zone has been the same all game!"* I probably would have yelled. I could have even topped it off with, *"That's your first warning,"* or some other kind of "pedestal phrase". Years ago, I believed responses like that actually helped; it showed the shortstop that I was on top of my game.

That shortstop was using a **Defender Comment**. His pitcher was upset and felt bad. Everyone noticed. He tried to pin it on the ump to defend his teammate, because that's what teammates and coaches do (more Self-Serving Bias). My biggest mistake would have been *responding* to that Defender Comment.

Some Defender Comments are so common, they become catchphrases:

>  *"Looked like a clean play from over here!"*
>  *"Pitch looked good to me!"*
>  *"Yeah, he's been calling them weird all day . . ."*
>  *"What do you expect from this ump?"*

Often your best response is to smile and move on.

Don't get us wrong; if someone approaches you with a specific info question about the game—how many fouls they get before they foul out—and you smile and walk away, that *is* actually bad customer service. That will piss people off.

If you are engaged with the game, moving and communicating, you will hear *everything*, including things that *are not meant for you*:

Defender Comments and complaints.

**Hearing everything because you're into the game is good. Responding to everything you hear is really, really bad, and will just distract you from the core habit.**

KEY CONCEPT

When a player asks:

> *"Ref, are you trying to cost my team the game?"*

Recognize that this is a Defender Comment, and not the beginning of a real conversation the player wants to have with you. What will your response be here? The Customer Service land version is:

> *"No sir, I am doing my best and I am sorry if you didn't like that last call, but that's what the rulebook says."*

Move on quickly from these fake questions, insults, and throw-away lines:

> *"Ref, you owe us one!"*
> *"Ump, you are missing a great game out here!"*
> *"Where is the instant replay on that one?"*

I used to think these comments all needed an instant response. In the beginning, every single comment seems amazingly important. Your *game info* and CCS is actually important when you first start.

Conflict and arguments are part of the job, but apologies have their place, too.

**Ref Myth:** I can never admit I'm wrong, or say, "I'm sorry," or else I will look weak!

**Ref Truth:** "Apologizing at the right time can actually help, and build your credibility."

REF MYTH

That's a direct quote from Mike Carey, one of my all-time favorite NFL refs. One day, years back, I was lucky enough to meet him, and he shared that surprising idea with me.

At the time, I was terrified to ever "apologize" for a reffing mistake. After that, I slowly started to try it out. I still wouldn't come right out during a game and say, "*Yeah, sorry I blew that call at second base.*" But maybe after the game—if the player is still questioning the call—I might say something like, "*Yeah, I would love another look at that second base call.*" That's a subtle way of saying, "*Yup—probably messed that one up,*" and gaining back some credibility.

The phrase, "***That's my bad***" has entered my Script Sheet as I get older and learn from smarter refs like Mike Carey.

**SCRIPT SHEET**

**Question #5 for your Script-Sheet:** how you will respond to a player when you realize that you made a mistake?

Personally I think I am right about 90% of the time. Meaning 1 out of every 10 calls I make is probably wrong. I'm a B+ Ref. What do you think your percentage will be?

Address legitimate questions and comments about game info; ignore Defender Comments and throw-away questions that are really insults. Be prepared to be wrong, have a good response in the moment, and *maybe* apologize in the right situation and in the right way. You can't default to an apology any time someone is unhappy with any call or decision. Just because a call generates CAP and players are unhappy doesn't mean it was the wrong decision and needs an instant apology.

Some apologies actually make things worse:

> "*I'm sorry you feel that way.*"
> "*I'm sorry if that's upsetting to you, but it's the right call.*"

These are actually **escalators**, which we will discuss in the next Key Habit.

For now, realize that a traditional customer service approach will turn you into a Squirrel Ref, where you race from issue to question to comment, trying to make everyone happy, apologizing for every single call, and taking your focus off what really matters: becoming the scoreboard and mastering your CCS.

# The Worst Game You Ever Ref

Beginning refs think the worst game they will ever ref is a "meltdown" game well into their career: nothing goes right, every play ends in an argument, and they end up quitting or getting yanked off the schedule.

The worst game you ever ref actually comes early—game five or six of your first fifteen. Most people don't realize it even happened.

The score of the softball or kickball game is 13-2. The football game is 42-14. The basketball game is 85-45.

You are barely tested, and halfway through, neither team is playing hard. So you abandon some of the habits that you just started forming. You stop announcing your CCS; you ease off on the frequency switch and your 3-Rep habit.

You don't notice when you miss a run, or when the volunteer at the scorer's table misses a free throw. You write down an incorrect score on your clipboard and forget to announce it, so no one helps you catch a simple scoring mistake.

You stop giving warnings about contact, or using the safety base, or pitching too fast, or any of the other teaching ideas that are part of the Teaching and Coaching slice of the 5 Jobs.

**TEACHER & COACH**

Maybe you even decide to stop using your scorebook or your ump clicker, and stop flashing the outs to the pitcher; you will just **try to remember** what's important. Become the scoreboard? Heck, it doesn't matter at this point; *this is all just for fun*.

A couple of players notice the score is off, but they don't say anything because it's a blow-out.

And guess what happens?

NOTHING HAPPENS!

The winning and losing teams come up and shake your hand afterwards. You stand proudly on the field thinking, *"What a great game–no controversy, no big arguments, and I even got some compliments! Sweet!"*

Except this game really just flipped a lot of brain switches back to the left, and inserted a bunch of bugs into your system that will soon be the origin of your meltdown game.

Fast forward twenty games—maybe this time it's the playoffs—and you miss that run scoring, except this time the score is not 13-2, but 8-7, and the losing teams swears you have the wrong score in the bottom of the sixth inning. The whole game comes to a halt. Everyone is talking in your ear and seems mad at you.

Players are also angry at each other—yelling across the field—because the warnings, teaching, and coaching you never gave during that blowout are now *necessary* in this close playoff game. You don't have the 3-Rep and CCS habits locked down; after every Coin-Flip Call, you instantly start worrying about getting yelled at and forget to mark down a score, or record and out, or change the down. Your avoidable scoreboard confusion gets worse.

The game ends in a controversial call that really only cropped up because you messed up the time and timeouts long ago. Even though one team wins, both teams are angry, and nobody comes up to shake your hand after this game; they are too busy grabbing their phones to text the league administrator and complain. You stand on the field alone after the game with that sinking feeling.

This story is very real, and has happened many times. We don't want to scare you, just prepare you.

As I was writing this section, I watched a Saturday afternoon kickball tournament game spiral out of control—yelling, cursing, even an ejection. The winning captain came over after the game and was STILL COMPLAINING! I have the whole thing on video tape.

Was he complaining about a close play at the plate? A random rule application? Mean-spirited play?

No. He was furious because in the sixth inning, the ump called three outs when there were actually only two.

**KEY CONCEPT**

**If you only start using your habits and systems when games are tough and close, you will quickly find you have no system to use.**

**REVERSAL**

The Beginner Brain always thinks that big calls create trust and credibility. So it's always looking for the big call and big moment, to show the players you are truly a ref! **As with many beginning ideas, the reverse is true.**

Teaching, tips and advice, hustle, reliable game info, and engagement all combine to create a positive balance in your **credibility bank**. The big moment—the huge, close call at the end of the game—that's when you spend the "credibility bucks" that you have been collecting from the very first play.

Make sure you actually have a balance, earning it through communication and consistent game info.

When you wreck your game info, you wreck the start of the engagement circle, and guarantee that when a big call needs to be made, your credibility bank will be at zero.

The path to becoming a great ref can be simple.

Refs who consistently give out good game info also signal and move better, make better calls, have good games, nice compliments, and long careers.

Refs that mess up info—that don't move and are rarely engaged—seem to make more bad calls, have more problems, receive more complaints, and never seem to last very long.

Fight the real villains that will distract you in the survival phase: the remember trap, the customer service trap, habit stress, and reffing small. Get on top of your game info, practice the one kick of your CCS, and become the scoreboard.

# Call Your Granny...

The best habits are sometimes boring, and silly to watch. Some people miss a chance to get better, because they are afraid to look a little goofy.

Just ask Wilt Chamberlain.

In "The Big Man Can't Shoot", an episode of Malcolm Gladwell's *Revisionist History* podcast, Gladwell points out a forgotten part of Wilt Chamberlain's record-setting 100-point basketball game:

Chamberlain made 28 of 32 free-throws during the game, and all twenty-eight of them were "granny shots"—underhanded shots tossed with two hands on the ball.

**GRANNY SHOT**

Chamberlain had the **highest free throw percentage of his entire career** the year of that hundred-point game—when he was shooting granny shots.

After Wilt became world famous with his hundred-point game, he promptly. . . stopped using his "granny shot". His free throw percentage fell about 15%, never again approaching his "granny year" percentage.

Maybe in the worst game you ever ref, you drop a habit that made you 15% better because it also made you look silly.

**New refs want to start with cool gear and signals when they should be finding simple granny shots.**

**KEY IDEA**

One of my favorite "granny shots" for new flag football refs who are struggling to master their CCS: Signal the down high in the air with your hand, and then drop that hand by your side while still holding the down number throughout the play.

You can do this for almost any sport. *What was the last down? How many outs?* Look at your hand!

It may look kind of silly, but we care about being *effective* more than *looking silly*. New refs will do this when they first start, then often ditch it once they pass the first fifteen games.

We tend to feel a lack of confidence when we think we look silly, but "granny shots" can actually *build* confidence if you're brave enough to try them out.

One day after a very close play, my Ref Brain took over and created a "**point first**" granny shot: before the call was clear in my mind, I moved toward—and *pointed at*—the spot where the action occurred to buy time. The point functions like the "hourglass" graphic or spinning wheel you see on a computer when it's taking a little longer to load: you see movement—*something* is happening—so you are less likely to become impatient or bail out completely.

On close coin-flip plays, you will often see Social Refs pointing at the action as a trigger to move into a decision, much like the "flamingo stance." Do they have the call already or are they buying time? If they are moving, engaged, and eventually get there, does it matter? When I have gotten caught out of position in the past, moving to the spot where the action happened—while pointing—and then reffing BIG has helped keep credibility with players.

Having trouble with a quick whistle? Trying pointing first to trigger your whistle. I often tell whistle happy new refs: *"Don't blow the whistle unless you can point at the reason you blew the whistle."*

**STOP & SQUASH**

One warning: **point at plays and action, not at people**. I try to never point at a player when talking to them. Even when a call is specifically 'on' someone, it's normally better to be vague (*the call was on the left side of the line*) than point them out. Pointing out a person is the same as calling them out—an Auto-CAP generator.

Try out the point-engagement technique, try holding numbers "in your hand," try developing your own granny shots to help simplify things in your survival phase, and don't be afraid to look a little silly!

*Simple Granny Shot in action: 2 outs being "held" in the right hand.*

## PHASE 3 RECAP

How will you ref when everything is going great?

Will you let your guard down? Ditch your habits and start 'trying to remember' everything? Abandon your tools and your CCS? Will you ref your "worst game ever" and not even know it?

Or will you keep your foot on the gas, embrace your game info, and build the info habits to become the scoreboard?

**KEY IDEAS:**

- Engagement starts with answering the core question: *What game info do the players need to know from me every play or every time there is action?*

- The "core habit" is delivering that game info to your players before they even ask you. This is the first step to becoming the scoreboard.

- Game info is the glue that connects everything for a new ref:

  > Your communication with players
  > Your credibility and trust
  > Your communication with other refs
  > Your engagement in the game
  > Your ability to announce the scoreboard as an automatic habit and move on to your other responsibilities

- Avoid falling into a **One-and-Done habit**, since most players won't hear or understand you the first time.

- Try using a **3-Rep Habit** to up the frequency on your game info (think of photos on a cellphone—you might take four or five pictures to get *one* winner).

- Game info is about frequency AND priority. The most important sequence of game info that can start and finish every play is your Core Communication Sequence (CCS).

- Remembering is not a system. It's what you do when you are missing habits to build a system.

- When in doubt, track your game info on tools like clickers, mini-scoreboards, and scorebooks.

- Avoid additional stress and wasted time by keeping track of your ref gear and your game info.

- Try to develop Universal Habits and Solutions: Ideas you communicate and actions you complete *every time* there is a trigger, so the focus is on feeling something missing, rather than "remembering" to get started.

- "Reffing Small" means your volume, speed and repetition, signals, and movement don't line up with the closeness or importance of the call in front of you.

- Don't become a "Squirrel Ref" trying to make every player happy. Not every comment or question needs a response. Not every complaint needs an apology.

- In the worst game you ever ref, you relax and stop building the simple habits that help you communicate game info and become the scoreboard.

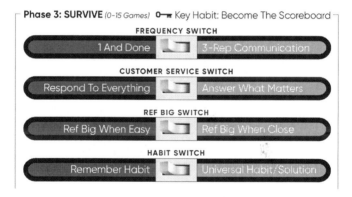

**Phase 3: SURVIVE** *(0-15 Games)*  Key Habit: Become The Scoreboard

FREQUENCY SWITCH

1 And Done · 3-Rep Communication

CUSTOMER SERVICE SWITCH

Respond To Everything · Answer What Matters

REF BIG SWITCH

Ref Big When Easy · Ref Big When Close

HABIT SWITCH

Remember Habit · Universal Habit/Solution

## Practice

Do you have a CCS? Practice all of the versions of it in front of a mirror.

Turn the volume off during a televised game and ref the game live with a whistle, your announcements, and big hand signals.

Develop some simple "Granny Shots" to help you engage in the game and become the scoreboard, even if they look silly.

# KEY HABIT: BECOME A DEFUSER

We have started the key habit of announcing game info and taken ownership of the scoreboard. Now we want to stabilize our communication system. We've talked about important ways to see calls better, and make the call more decisively. Now let's deal with communication once a decision has been made, and people aren't happy!

In the "Stabilize" phase, we will focus on the 4th Habit: **Becoming a Defuser** in tense and stressful CAP situations.

There is a 3-part framework when learning to defuse CAP and arguments:

1. **Don't make the situation worse.**
2. **Check that players actually understand the issue.**
3. **Try to defuse the situation with your toolbox.**

We will introduce some common defuser villains, talk about fault and perspective, look at bad apples and Kryptonite, and give you a starting toolbox you can use to defuse.

## The Honk

*Seattle. WA, 2011.* Driving a half-mile from home, I notice something strange out of the corner of my eye: a guy on the sidewalk seems to hop up in the air and then instantly fall down on the ground.

I slow my car down, looking in the rear-view mirror.

*Yeah, this guy is definitely laying down on the sidewalk. Not good. I should probably pull a U-turn up at the next—*

**HONK HONK HONK HONK HOOOOOOOONK!**

A dude in the car behind me is laying on the horn and blaring awful

Techno music.

I have extended his travel-time to the World's Biggest Douchebag (WBD) contest by at least ten seconds. He pulls his black car with neon lights alongside mine, and with his window rolled down, yells *"F*CK YOU A**HOLE!"* and flips me the bird, before gunning his engines and racing off.

This is not a busy street.

I whip my car around and realize that this poor young skinny guy on the sidewalk is bleeding from his head. I call 911 and an ambulance is there in minutes. Unfortunately, the young guy has just suffered the first seizure of his life. I explain what I saw to the head paramedic, they whisk the guy away, and soon I'm back on the way home.

But I'm thinking about TechnoGuy, and reffing.

What do you say about someone who leans on the horn and flips you the bird when you are trying to help a seizure victim on the sidewalk?

The Beginner Brain gets mad, because someone else is honking mad. Your Ref Brain sees the other perspective first and understands that the other person might not know any better.

TechnoGuy has no idea why I was stopped in the middle of the street. Maybe from his perspective, I was actually being a dangerous driver.

What would you say to TechnoGuy if you were in the car when he flipped us off? Do you have a good response in mind?

More importantly, would it have helped? Or would it have instantly made the situation worse? Would it have distracted us from helping the poor skinny dude?

Sometimes in life you do what's right, smart, and safe, and still get conflict. You are 100% right, but others don't know that; they don't see the guy on the sidewalk. All they see is your car in their way of what matters to them in the moment.

Can you be calm and patient enough to wait out their honking?

You have probably had a few moments like this in your life, and you will have many more on the field.

You will be trying to teach or help a team, when a different kind of TechnoGuy will yell out, *"THIS BETTER NOT BE COMING OUT OF OUR TIME!"*

You will have moments when you call a penalty or foul, and one team is so quick to start yelling and complaining, they don't even realize you called it on the other team.

A team once yelled at me to *"HURRY UP!"* as I was helping up an injured player who hurt her knee.

These moments used to make me furious; now I just try to smile.

**All defusion starts with a basic idea: First, avoid making things worse.**

**KEY CONCEPT**

Your Beginner Brain is probably wired with comebacks and responses to CAP that will instantly make things worse, no matter what the sport. They will make your communication harder, make your games less fun, and make your five jobs feel like a drag.

To defuse, you need to stop responding to insults and attacks about your decisions—even when someone else gets personal.

That's hard. That goes against human nature. The Beginner Brain wants to defend quick and react FAST!

> *You attack me; I fight back. You insult me; I turn it right around. You honk at me; I flip you the bird.*

Great Social Refs wait out the honking. They learn to pivot and defuse instead. They don't get stuck in melt-down arguments that derail their games and their day.

**Social Refs don't get trapped in battles that never need to be fought in the first place.**

**KEY IDEA**

They realize that some honks, attacks, and insults come from situations when you just have more info and understanding than the other person.

# The "Fake" Defuser

A funny scene plays out often during our auditions with new refs.

Someone will make a sweeping statement:

> *"I'm really good with people and dealing with conflict."*

*"Awesome,"* we reply. *"Let's see what you can do!"*

We run the candidate through a role-playing situation: an angry player upset about an obvious penalty.

Eight times out of ten, their response to the angry player is always some version of:

**ESCALATOR**

*"Sir, just CALM DOWN and LISTEN for a second!"*
*"Just RELAX. I don't know what you're getting angry about–that was an easy call."*
*"YOU fouled him; don't get ANGRY at me. Just make a better play next time."*

How do you think those responses will work on the field?

**Narrator's Voice:** *"They work very poorly."*

In any CAP situation, there are a host of things you can say and do, but your response will fall into two clear cut categories:

**ESCALATOR**

Your response will **Escalate** the situation—make people more confused, pissed-off, and upset.

**DEFUSER**

Your response will **Defuse** the situation—calm things down and keep them from getting worse.

New refs instinctively race in with **Fake Defusers**, thinking they are helping put out the fire, when they really have a can full of gasoline.

Throughout the history of the universe, shouting, "CALM DOWN" has never calmed anyone down.

Telling someone to "RELAX" or "CHILL OUT" usually has the opposite effect.

Beyond these initial instincts, there are tons more Fake Defusers that you will hear other refs use–things you might end up saying yourself without even thinking.

**ESCALATOR**

*"Get over it, it's just kickball/flag football/dodgeball/ (whatever sport.)"*

*"It's not that big of a deal. I don't know why you're getting so upset."*

*"Everyone saw you do it. Let it go."*

**Fake Defusers** have 3 main traits:

> **They make sense in your head, but never really help.**
>
> **They feel personal, like scolding or criticism.**
>
> **They often feel really good and easy to say as an instant reaction.**

Fake Defusers are **dismissive**. They make it seem like you don't care, and it makes players feel like you aren't interested in listening to them.

What they are saying could be absolutely wrong and totally crazy, but you're not going to change human behavior or opinions, and there is no "winning" when it comes to arguments or battles with players. There is no winning debates, because there is no "absolute truth" on the field, just perspectives of the three games.

Try To Win & Change Minds  Defuse & Pivot

Many CAP battles never need to happen in the first place. Notice and eliminate Fake Defusers you use in normal conversation, so you don't end up using them on the field.

As a practice exercise, quickly circle all of the **Fake Defusers** below:

*"You need to take a second and relax."*

*"I can make the calls here–that's why I am the ref and you are the player."*

*"Everyone saw what you did; it was really obvious."*

*"You know that you pushed him–stop arguing with us."*

*"The penalty is 100% on you. Next time try and be more careful."*

*"You're wrong; that's not what happened during the play."*

*"Instead of complaining, make a better play next time."*

*"You know you aren't supposed to do that."*

*"You should go read the rulebook if that's what you think."*

*"What do you expect me to do about it?"*

*"It's not my fault/problem that you guys don't know the rules."*

*"You are just wasting everyone's time by arguing something so obvious."*

Maybe you already caught onto the trick. They are *all* Fake Defusers. We have heard every one of them over the years. A big part of turning on your Ref Brain is ditching all of these old default responses that will actually make your job harder.

As a ref, instant calls and reactions to plays are good. Instant reaction to conflict generated by those plays and calls is normally bad. Instant reactions to "feeling attacked" lead to bad comebacks, and bad results.

# Don't Ride the Escalator

In addition to Fake Defusers, there are four common "escalator instincts" that will lead to more problems:

## The Ignore Instinct

Many new refs have a common reaction to their first heated situation: they just ignore it and walk away. If you ignore a player at the first sign of CAP, you will likely make the situation worse.

If a frustrated player asks you, *"Why was that pass interference?"* or, *"What did I do wrong there?",* your first response should be to **explain what you saw**.

Ignoring someone never calms them down. Just think of your own experiences.

> *"I was really upset that the store wouldn't help me fix my cellphone, but once they ignored me for five minutes I felt much better and saw their side of the story."*

Everyone likes to be heard. No one likes to be ignored. Engage with legitimate questions and confusion, and don't ignore someone just because they are visibly upset or angry.

## Honest Abe Instinct

Every ref should be honest, but there is such a thing as being *too* honest. When dealing with angry players, often new refs will focus on "responsibility" to try and get out of the situation.

> *"That's not my call to make."*
>
> *"You need to talk to the other ref."*
>
> *"I can't do anything about that/What do you want me to do about it?"*

These can all be true, but they will make your situation worse. You may not have seen the play. You may not be able to make the call. You might be dealing with a complaint about a call that is another ref's responsibility.

You don't need to *say* that!

This "too-honest" approach can also combine with other ideas like the over-apology:

> *"I'm sorry, I must have missed that. I am new here—it's my first day!"*

Taking responsibility for your field and your calls is great, but dang—don't be *that* honest, or it will be a long day.

Honesty can also contribute to the most common default reaction to an angry player:

> *"I didn't see it."*

Teams can be mad about a call or decision you made, and they can also be mad about something you missed. . . something they felt was obvious as can be, and they were counting on you to notice.

A player comes up to you super upset:

> *"Ref, this dude is totally grabbing me every play."*

Try a very simple start:

**Squash "I didn't see it" and substitute "I didn't HAVE it."**

"I didn't HAVE it," will give you much more flexibility. It conveys ownership, and also the idea that for many "controversial or contact" plays you will see exactly what the player was asking about, and CHOOSE to not make a call.

Players see what they want to see. Sometimes the biggest arguments of all come from the simplest of actions: **a player falling down on the ground**. When you learn to see the Third Game, you can start to see when situations don't require a call. When you are watching the 1st game like a spectator, every time someone falls down, they were pushed, knocked down or fouled.

> *"Ref, did you not see my player get knocked down right there?"*

**Practice: How would a Beginner Brain respond?**

> *"No, you're wrong. She didn't get knocked over."*

**Practice: How should your Ref Brain respond?**

> *"I didn't have a foul there, looked like the player stumbled and fell down."*

"I didn't have it on that play. . ." or, "I see what you mean, but I didn't have a foul/penalty" is a better way to communicate. It gives you more options to defuse a situation.

## YES-NO Responses ("Oppo" Responses)

This instinct is really, *really* hard to turn off. I *still* struggle with it often.

A YES-NO (or "oppo" response) occurs when you immediately respond to a player's statement with the opposite of what they just said using "yes" or "no":

> "Ref, that was a Flag Guard!"
> "**NO**, that wasn't a Flag Guard!"

"Ref, that wasn't pass interference."
"**YES**, it was totally interference."

> "Ump, she is pitching too fast!"
> "**NO**, that pitch is not too fast!"

They may be wrong and you may be right, but it's still a lousy way to respond to players, as it **immediately dismisses everything they just said**.

Your Beginner Brain wants to fire back a response *as fast as possible* to defend itself, but this will lead to getting trapped in an endless cartoon CAP loop:

**ESCALATOR**

"Yes, you did."
"No, I didn't."
"Oh, yes you did."
"OH, NO I DIDN'T."
"DID!"
"DIDN'T!"

These loops just escalate situations.

Instead, respond to definitive criticism from players with a brief explanation, as opposed to a YES-NO.

> *"Ref, that was a Flag Guard!"*
> **"Yeah, looked like the flag was pulled before the flag guard happened."**

> *"Ump, she is pitching too fast."*
> **"That speed is still okay. I will keep an eye on it."**

Responding with information—instead of the opposite of what a player just said—will get you going down the escalator towards the defuser department.

## The Killer Comeback!

I'm working a game as the only kickball ump and for some reason one team's catcher won't leave me alone They make a comment after every pitch, and seem really unhappy about something.

In our kickball league, sometimes we make "delayed calls". The ump raises their arm to signify a call is coming, but the call is determined like "advantage" in soccer. After one play where I have my arm up but don't call anything because it *benefits* the defense, the catcher makes a rude comment, and I instantly go into a "**killer comeback**":

> **"See this arm in the air, CATCHER?"** *(I am pointing at my own raised arm with the other hand.) I see exactly what you want me to call, except that I'm not stopping the game because it **BENEFITS** your team! Want me to take that OUT off the board for your team, and redo the play???"*

The catcher mumbles something about not understanding and quiets down.

> *"Yes!"* I think. *"Job well done!"*

But for a Social Ref, more like, "**job poorly done**".

Maybe you've had this experience officiating. Or maybe you have done something similar to a friend or family member. Here's how it feels in real-time:

> **One minute later:** *Yes, I finally said what was on my mind and nailed them!*
> **Five minutes later:** *Whew, that felt GOOD! Glad I did that.*
> **Fifteen minutes Later:** *Hmmm, doesn't feel quite as good as it did ten minutes ago.*
> **One hour later:** *There's a possibility I could have handled that differently.*
> **Three hours later:** *Yeah, I definitely should have said something different there.*
> **Twelve hours later (In bed, staring at ceiling):** *Man, that was really stupid. I wish I didn't say what I did. Maybe I should apologize.*
> **Twenty-four hours later:** *I am a moron. I have to make sure I never say that again.*

It should be no surprise that the next day the office got an email from the catcher, basically calling me out for being a lousy, super-rude umpire and asking that I never ump their games again.

There will be many chances for you to instantly respond to angry players with your own sweet insult or **killer comeback**.

Don't do it. This is *the* hardest Beginner Brain instinct to break.

If you are really excited about what you are going to say in response to conflict or an insult—if you are almost giddy to get the response out—then **don't say it**.

If it feels like your killer comeback will put the player in their place and shut them down, it will probably do the opposite, and prolong the conflict.

**If a comeback or comment feels really good to say to a player, PLEASE don't say it!**

**Ref Myth:** If I don't push back and defend my calls, then I will be seen as weak and the players will walk all over me!

**Ref Truth:** You earn *more* respect and credibility by smiling and remaining unfazed by player insults and anger.

A few years after that kickball game, I read the great book, Verbal Judo by George J. Thompson. This classic line is from the chapter perfectly entitled, "Taking Crap with Dignity. . . and Style":

**"Never use words that rise readily to your lips, or you'll make the greatest speech you ever live to regret."**

As soon as I read that line, I thought of my conversation with that kickball catcher.

It's instinctive to want to defend yourself. To stand up to someone attacking you. . . your brain is calculating responses every time someone insults you and does you wrong.

**Anger is easy.**

Anger is an easy way out of a situation. It's much harder to understand, teach and have empathy. How would that catcher know what my raised arm meant? How could they know I was on their side, and actually helping them, by raising my arm? They talk about delayed calls in the rulebook, but. . . we already know that nobody reads that thing.

**Most disagreements never need to crown a winner.**

If you need to keep getting the last word and lecturing people on how correct you are with killer comebacks, you'll end up being the most correct person that no one ever wants near their games.

When dealing with conflict, the Beginner Brain loves ideas that are quick and easy shortcuts that feel awesome in the moment. Those responses always escalate situations, and make your job harder.

# Make Sure They Understand You

Confusion is an Escalator. Clarity can help defuse.

We've talked about how reffing small can create confusion, but let's talk about two more concepts that will block your ability to communicate clearly.

## Classroom Talk vs Field Talk

There is a story that Dr. Seuss wrote the famous children's book, *Green Eggs and Ham* to win a bet with his editor: could he write a book using only fifty common words? The bet was for $50—a buck a word.

*Green Eggs and Ham* went on to sell 8 million copies, probably because every kid in America found it easy and understandable.

When you learn your rulebook, you will be flooded with all kinds of fancy terms that most people won't understand. Heavy words like "illegal," "ineligible," "intentional," and "inadvertent". Your league probably has its own special language and terms. If you have formal training, it normally takes place in a classroom setting, with charts and rules, Power Points and long explanations.

**Classroom Talk** is how someone teaches you the format and rules of your league.

When you hit the field or the court, you want your communication to be **raw, simple, and clear**. You don't have time for fancy words or long detailed explanations.

You need **Field Talk**.

SIMPLE TALK SWITCH
Classroom Talk | Field Talk

Many refs learn their sport through Classroom Talk, and then try and re-use that Classroom Talk on the field. This is another example of the "Curse of Knowledge": because you know more than the players, it's hard to simplify what you want to say.

Classroom Talk doesn't work with players and fans. You are moving with the speed of the game in real time. You don't have time for complexity, and the players won't understand you anyway. You need to talk less like a college professor, and more like Dr. Seuss. If you constantly use rule book language and phrases that nobody understands, you will just end up escalating situations.

Underdog has a unique safety rule for our flag football leagues called the Box Rule—basically 3 yards and in on the goal-line, you draw an imaginary line 3 yards on either side of the line of scrimmage marker, and then draw the line towards the goal-line. The offense can't run the ball through that area or else it's a penalty.

Understand the Box Rule now? Probably not! Most people have a hard time understanding Classroom Talk.

Often when you announce first, goal, and Box Rule, a player will ask, "*What's the Box Rule?*" because they don't read the rulebook!

I've watched new refs try to explain the entire background of the Box Rule in between plays. You can understand the instinct, because that's exactly how they were taught in the classroom.

When I get asked about the Box Rule, I just say:

> "*Don't run up the middle.*"

Now do you understand the Box Rule better?

That's Field Talk, because in that moment, getting ready for the next play, that's all anyone can digest.

I've watched refs confuse teams before a game even started because they over-complicated the choice of "home and away" or "offense or defense" with Classroom Talk. We literally decide these things with Rock-Paper-Scissors before the game, and yet afterward, the ref is throwing out phrases like, "*deferring your choice*" and "*Which end zone do you select to defend?*"

How about:

> "*Do you want to bat first, or last?*"
> "*Want the ball to start the first half, or the second half?*"

The players don't need to understand the background and philosophy of every rule. . . just get to the point. It's easy to just say everything you know—it's harder to use just a few words, and talk in simple and clear language to players who are new and confused. Don't create additional problems by bringing classroom talk to the field.

## Negative Communication Patterns

Richard Nixon might have been before your time, but you have probably heard one of his most famous quotes:

*"I am NOT a crook!"*

Of course he turned out to be a huge crook, and resigned in disgrace. The question is: Does telling someone what you *ARE NOT* actually help or hurt?

The newspaper handled Nixon's famous quote like this:

If you were walking down the street and quickly saw the front page in a store, what would be your first impression?

I see: **President** and **Crook**.

You will see this in writing, in media, in your everyday conversation: people telling you what *didn't* happen, or what they *are NOT*, or generally talking in circles when there is a much easier—and more direct—way of saying something. (I am sure there are a few Easter Eggs hiding in this book!)

The patterns are full of "not," "don't," "can't," and "won't".

Your friend asks, *"Can we go to the store?"*

You can say: *"I don't see any reason why we can't go to the store."*

Or you can say: *"Yeah, let's go to the store."*

You see these strange communication patterns crop up in lots of sports situations, often from "expert" commentators:

> *"There isn't anything that Jane the Superstar can't do on the tennis court."*

This is an actual quote I read—from a staff writer—on ESPN.com one day:

> *"Jerry Jones said there is no consideration not having Tony Romo on the roster going past this season."*

Eh? Is he going to be on the roster? What about:

> *"Jerry Jones said that Tony Romo will definitely be on the roster next season."*

New refs will let these misleading communication patterns creep into their calls and explanations.

> "NOT a **Strike**"
> "There was NO **catch** on the play"
> "NOT a **Fair Ball**"

Fields and courts are large places. When a beginner is reffing small and failing to use enough volume, negative communication patterns will ALWAYS be misunderstood.

People focus on key words, like **President** and **Crook**. They seldom focus on filler words like "no," "not," and "don't". The people on your field will just hear:

> "**Strike**"
> ". . .**Catch** on the play"
> "**Fair** Ball"

When you keep using negative qualifiers in your phrases, you run the risk of being constantly misunderstood.

Sometimes new refs default to being "polite," right back to the customer service trap. It's always nicer to tell someone that their work is "not so great" instead of saying "it's bad!" Gentler to tell a player they "did not quite achieve the first down" then to say "turnover on downs." Avoid being "polite" when it means being indirect and using negative communication patterns that will just confuse players.

Remember the "**echoing**" benefit when you become the scoreboard—players will echo back your game info. When you use negative patterns, players will echo those back too:

> *"Okay, sorry guys, but this is NOT a GENDER play!"* you say in a co-rec league.

> *"Guys, GENDER play coming up here!"* the defense instantly echoes back.

I've actually heard a kickball ump say: *"The ball didn't come in slow enough, so it wasn't a strike!"*

How about: ***"Too fast, pitcher. Ball One!"***

> Good news—there is a name for something that's NOT a Strike: it's a **Ball**!

> There is a name for something that is NOT a catch: it's an **incompletion**!

> There is a name for something that was NOT a Fair Ball: it's a **FOUL Ball**! <always yell FOUL, always signal FAIR!>

And there is a phrase for someone who is NOT a crook: "I am **innocent**!"

Switch your brain from the habit of explaining what did NOT happen to explaining what actually DID happen to communicate more like a Social Ref.

BOOK COVER

## *Book Cover Break:*
## *Avoid the 4 Body Language Bugs*

Bad body language is another escalator.

Social Refs tend to keep their hands and body open when talking with players.

STOP & SQUASH

New refs instinctively make fists with their hands, point at players, and make pounding or chopping motions with one hand on top of the other.

Avoid these **4 Body Language Bugs** that directly involve your hands and arms:

**1**. **Crossing your arms across your chest:** This pose—"The Bouncer"— shows conflict and a lack of interest. If you want to cross your arms, try "The Morpheus" pose of crossing them behind your back. Crossing your arms during a play, or when talking to players, is a surefire escalator.

ESCALATOR

"The Bouncer"

"The Morpheus"

DEFUSER

**2. Hands on your hips:** This is another natural instinct, but it shows unhappiness and impatience. Shift your weight onto one of your hips and it looks even worse. Keep your hands off your hips.

**3. Hands in your pockets:** A common default position for many rookie refs. If it's 20 degrees outside and you are freezing, okay, put your hands in your pockets. Otherwise squash that bug; it makes you look bored and disengaged.

**4. The Shrug:** There are two kinds of shrugs—the Hand Shrug, and the Full Shrug. Both drive players nuts because they send a message that you're helpless or lacking info. Avoid the shrug instinct.

For video examples of these book cover bugs in action, visit www.socialref.net/bookcover.

# Two Escalator Reversal Switches

We know the main ways we can confuse people and escalate issues on the field. Let's talk about switches that you will need to flip to start defusing common situations.

When people don't like or understand your call, there is a natural instinct to keep explaining. Usually after one or two quick **Field Talk** explanations, the more you try and explain yourself and your decision, the *worse* you make the situation, especially when you just repeat the same thing over and over again.

It doesn't help teach; it's really just a different way of saying, *"Let me tell you AGAIN why I am right, and you are wrong."*

Refs in the Stabilize Phase tend to get stuck in the Over-Explanation or TMI trap. Someone disagrees with your call, so you try and explain it to them multiple ways, but you're never really clarifying anything, just making them more frustrated. You are treating them like they can't HEAR you instead of dealing with the idea that they don't UNDERSTAND you.

Maybe you have seen this happen in another country: a tourist asks a native speaker for directions to a restaurant or the bathroom. The person doesn't understand the question. So the tourist just repeats the same exact question LOUDER, as if volume would solve the language problem.

Your problem is that players hate the call, and don't understand what they did wrong. Unless you're a master diplomat, there are very few times when explaining a call, in more detail, will make the person like it better, or see your side.

Frequency is your friend for game info and becoming the scoreboard. Frequency and over-explanation is your **enemy** for trying to defuse conflict when someone hates your call. The more you explain it, the angrier they get.

 **Over-explaining a call that no one likes is an escalator.**

KEY CONCEPT

Maybe you think, *"Well, if the player doesn't understand what I am saying, maybe I can SHOW them why I made the call. . ."*

**STOP & SQUASH**

**NEVER** re-enact plays, fouls, and penalties for players.

Your Beginner Brain thinks this will help to show them and tell them. 99% of the time, it will just piss them off even more. This is a bug you need to squash.

Try and show someone where an arm was, or where their feet were, and they just respond by saying:

> *"No, my arm was actually here," and "My feet were like this, not like that!"*

And on you go. . .

Over-explaining your calls is an escalator. Re-enacting the play is a MEGA-ESCALATOR! Don't do it. Switch your energy to repeating the game info, with the TMI switch.

Refs in the stabilize phase need a **Pivot Sequence**—a way to pivot from a situation where a player clearly doesn't like your call and explanation.

**SCRIPT SHEET**

**Question #6 for your Script Sheet:** After a couple of simple explanations, what pivot will you use when a player asks you to keep explaining your call?

Remember Jay? Just copy him:

> *"If you'd like, we can talk about it more at halftime, or during the next break."*

Don't dismiss. Pivot. Have a go-to line in your Script Sheet to move on from a situation when you have hit your max in explaining a tough decision.

PERSPECTIVE SWITCH

A guaranteed auto-escalator—much like the YES-NO loop—is telling a player they are guilty when *they* think they are innocent.

*"Ref, how can you make that call?"*
**"Easy, YOU pushed off with YOUR left arm."**
*"No, I didn't!"*
**"YES, you DID!"**

**ESCALATOR**

And away we go. . .

Honestly, I have seen enough "crazy pill" situations to realize there is something more going on here. There aren't THAT MANY bad liars in the world . . . I hope. Players that are caught up in the moment—running full speed and competing—instinctively do certain things that they don't even realize or remember: pushing off another player, hooking them, or grabbing onto a jersey.

That's no excuse—it can still be a foul, or a penalty. Directly accusing a player of an action never helps sell your call; it just escalates the situation. It makes them want to defend themselves in front of others, and it makes things personal when the player might not even realize they did something wrong.

Smart refs make the bad news they give to people a matter of perspective.

> *"Here is what **I saw** happen"* (vs. *"Here is what **you** 100% absolutely **did**"*).

It's a Beginner Brain instinct to tell someone what they did and add "**absolute qualifiers**" as support to help make your case:

*"You **DEFINITELY** pushed off. 100%. **NO DOUBT. ABSOLUTELY. CLEAR AS DAY!**"*

**STOP & SQUASH**

These qualifiers might make YOU feel better—like you are adding stronger evidence to your case—but they make everyone else feel worse. We are back to the origins of CAP: getting called out in front of friends and feeling criticized by the ref.

Great Social Refs often use the "**Historical Voice**"; they explain a situation like they are merely an observer:

> *"Looked to me like the arm was around the waist before the ball got there."*

> *"It was close, but I saw the front foot still up in the air when the ball got to first."*

Once you have flipped the Perspective Switch—from trying to tell someone exactly what **they did**, to explaining what **you saw**—realize that you're basically stating your opinion, and it's really hard to argue with someone's opinion. You can debate all day long about the best movie of all time, but it's harder to argue with someone about *their favorite* movie of all time. Maybe you hate *The Matrix*, or *Shawshank*, but if they are my favorites, then I just view them differently than you. You can still argue and make fun of me all day long, but that's MY perspective, and my opinion.

Start down-playing conflict with, *"here's what I saw"*. Then you can add on the Historical Voice, to take the person and "blame" out of the explanation and further defuse situations.

**Beginner Brain Explanation:** "YOU definitely hooked YOUR arm around his waist."

**Ref Perspective Explanation:** "From where I was, looked like you grabbed them around the waist before the ball got there."

**Historical Voice:** "Looked like the arm was around the receiver's waist before the ball got there."

These are subtle changes, YOUR arm to THE arm, but they make a HUGE difference over time. Try changing your explanations to a perspective-based opinion, to keep conflict from escalating.

# Bad Apples, Kryptonite, and Context

*"In a gathering of 7 or 8 people, we will surely meet one or two who like us a lot, and one or two who are not fond of us. Don't take it personally, this is the way of the world."*

—Haemin Sunim, *The Things You Can See Only When You Slow Down*

I hope we haven't scared you off with "crazy pill" stories and preparing you for conflict. Many players are really no problem at all in rec leagues. If we have spent too much time on CAP and arguments, it is because that's where you will need your habits and system the most. If everyone was honest and nice and played by every rule, maybe refs would be out of a job?

There are always going to be a few players who just want to argue and fight about everything—the smallest procedure, every call you are missing—anything they can do to throw you off your game. We call them **Bad Apples**. Who knows why they think it's fun to cause trouble and argue with the refs every play. Maybe they watched their favorite coach on TV get red-faced yelling at officials. Maybe they think it gives them an advantage with you. Maybe they think it's fun to constantly "bust your onions." Maybe they don't like you; maybe they love drama.

Bad Apples *do* like CAP, they like arguments, they like battling and pushing the envelope to see how much they can get away with. They will hopefully only be a fraction of what you have to deal with, but they do exist, so identify them quickly.

More importantly, don't build your communication habits around these Bad Apples, trying to change them or convert them. They are only pleased when you are rattled and making mistakes. They make trouble while claiming they are the victim.

Ignore them, isolate them, joke with them. Don't buy into their crap.

One day a Bad Apple was all over me, questioning every call, taking every break in the action to go back and debate a past decision. Finally during another debate about the tiniest issue, something clicked in my head and I decided to give it a try:

> "You know. . . I'm not going to eject you."

I didn't hear a word out of him for the rest of the game. I found out much later he had been ejected several times by other refs. . . maybe he liked the drama.

Also be aware of your **Kryptonite**: a player that talks or acts in a certain way that is guaranteed to drive you crazy. We have talked a lot about ways to defuse player anger, but most refs have at least one or two Kryptonites that really get in their head.

If you find yourself mentally replaying the way a player treated you or talked to you days or weeks after a game, then you have probably found your Kryptonite.

My Kryptonite is a catcher that starts talking while a softball pitch is in the air.

"*Wow, great pitch,*" they say as some junk pitch way outside comes towards the plate. We know why they do this—to try and get unconfident batters to swing at crap. I always say something, leading the catcher to drive me even more nuts:

> "Well, there is nothing in the rules that says I can't talk while the pitch is in the air!"

*So. . . many. . . responses. . . in. . . brain. . . must. . . .avoid. . . killer comeback!*

> "I agree; there is nothing in the rules. But maybe just for me today, please don't yell stuff while the ball is on the way to the plate."

Identify your Kryptonites so they don't derail your game and your day.

Know how you will deal with them before they even show up. It's normally not the person, it's the player profile. Even if you avoid a particular team or player, their profile will show up again if you ref long enough.

**Question #7 for your Script Sheet:** Who is your Kryptonite? Someone who questions your work ethic or your honesty? Someone who complains about safety, but is a really unsafe player? How will you handle them when you EVENTUALLY come across their path?

SCRIPT SHEET

Sometimes a player or whole team will turn into a Bad Apple VERY quickly based on the context of the game. Players you previously thought were your "friends" will flip on you fast in two common situations:

1. A team that is heavily favored and feels they SHOULD win starts losing and playing like crap (the 1-seed is down badly to the 8-seed in the playoffs).

2. A team that was cruising for an easy victory early blows a huge lead and the whole game "tenses up".

Players and teams in both situations will often pick a small play with no importance and seek to dump the whole game on your shoulders, sometimes even trying to disqualify themselves. It doesn't matter that the 1-seed threw 3 straight INT's in the first half. It will be a questionable TD call you make in the second half when the game is already lost that will have them trying to bite your head off.

These teams are venting. They SHOULD have won, they even felt the victory, and now it's gone. It's hard for most people to admit they blew it—Self Serving Bias and blaming you is easier. Teams that instantly flip to Bad Apples after blowing a huge lead or being dealt a huge upset are just dealing with normal human emotions. Fighting back against them will just make it worse.

Keep an eye out for Bad Apples and Kryptonites, and realize that huge upsets and point swings in rec sports leagues can cause people to flip to these traits quickly.

# The Defuser Toolbox

Your info habits and priorities can easily get pushed to the side by drama, anger, and insults, turning small things into big things. "Defusion" will be one of the most important components of your system.

Whether you realize it or not, you probably defuse tough situations in your life daily:

You change the subject when a crazy uncle wants to talk politics at Thanksgiving.

You comfort a crying kid who skinned her knee, asking her about a favorite toy or if she wants some ice cream.

You make a joke about yourself and what a screw-up you are when a sibling is sad or angry about bad news.

The ability to defuse revolves around three basic questions:

**DEFUSER**

**Does it seem like you are listening and you care?**

**Can you pivot from the original disagreement?**

**Can you disarm someone by complimenting them or just making them laugh?**

These three key questions will help outline an intro Defusion Toolkit of the best ideas you can start using.

## Listen and Support (Be a Fan)

It is easier for someone to take a call, a foul, a penalty—general bad news—if you seem like you actually hear what they have to say.

**Hearing someone's concerns does not mean you have to agree with them.**

Great Social Refs develop a unique ability to make it feel like they are agreeing with a player, while still deciding "against" them. A Social Ref like Jay always seemed to have a *"Yeah, I know, right?"* response ready for any situation. The agreement is more about being a fan of the player, and having their back than agreeing with their argument.

**DEFUSER**

*"What kind of stupid rule is that, ref?"*

**"Yeah, I know it's pretty confusing, but it only cost you 5 yards."**

*"They were totally safe at first base!"*

**"Yeah, I know it was super close, but looked like the throw got 'em."**

This kind of communication may take some time to develop, especially if you are always on the defensive and wasting energy on the next "killer comeback".

Another good way to show you are listening and supportive is to find one part of a complaint or argument you can agree with and include that in your response:

*"No way that was pass interference, ref; I got all ball!"*

**"I AGREE—the left hand definitely got the ball, but the right hand looked like it was on the arm."**

We use this idea often with Underdog Sports Leagues. We call it the "**one good thing rule**" from the book, *How to Win Friends and Influence People*: no matter how crazy or unreasonable a customer comment or complaint is, you can normally find one good point to agree with.

A team captain sends an email to the office that says, *"Your refs are terrible and biased and out to get us, and they started the game late and then ruled against us on every play, and they don't know the rules, and don't hustle, and are also terrible people and bad dancers."*

Response: *"We agree that game should not have started late. We will do better."*

If you can find a smaller point to agree with, you will have more credibility with players as they recognize that you are engaged and listening, instead of dismissing them. Players already won't like your rulings. When you dismiss every question and comment and skip finding "one good thing", you miss the chance to help defuse a situation.

**BOOK COVER**

## *Book Cover Break: Face Cues*

Your body and face are important when listening to players. Many new refs ruin the chance to build credibility because their body language and facial expressions make it look like they just don't care.

**Be careful about what your face communicates while you are talking, AND while you are listening.**

Frowns, squinting, smirking, rolling your eyes, big heavy sighs, and looking off to the side are all ways to give the impression that you aren't listening and could care less.

**STOP & SQUASH**

And please. . . let people finish. One of the quickest ways to drive a player nuts and escalate a situation is to start shaking your head slowly from side-to-side while they are talking to you.

This "shaking no" cue drives players nuts. Try hard to eliminate that instinct, even if a player or coach is 100% wrong.

**STOP & SQUASH**

[Visit www.socialref.net/BookCover to see examples of the frown and other facial cues and habits to avoid]

You can add a good facial cue to your Defuser Toolbox with a **Simple Start**: Visually agree with yourself.

**SIMPLE START**

Nod your head "yes" as you signal a big touchdown catch. Shake your head "no" as you signal a big incompletion or dropped catch at first base. No matter what you say and signal, your face normally tells a story.

## Pivot or Pause

When I was young and had the hiccups, my Mom took great pleasure in trying to scare the living crap out of me so they would go away. Maybe someone has tried doing this to you. It's an old wives' tale.

It persists because changing someone's focus and attention can sometimes be a valuable tool.

When someone has the hiccups, you don't normally say, "STOP HICCUPING!"

Yet when dealing with conflict from players, many refs try this same technique, only making things worse.

Scaring someone to distract them from the hiccups is a pivot. It's about breaking momentum. When players are angry and upset, and more and more teammates chime in to defend their friend, momentum can be your enemy.

The issue is players *believing* that you hear them and that you are engaged in the game. Refs get so stuck in the YES-NO loop trying to push back on an upset player that they miss the chance to pivot, acknowledge the player's concerns, and defuse a bad situation.

There is always a **future pivot** from a player complaint:

**SIMPLE START**

*"Ref, he totally grabbed my arm!"*

***"I didn't have it on that play. . . I will watch for it going forward."***

You can even get specific:

> *"Ref, they keep fouling/pushing/grabbing/insulting us every play!"*
>
> ***"Okay, I hear you—who should I watch for?"***

Asking a player to be specific and point out the player or thing that is making them unhappy is a key defusion element, but can only occur with a "**future pivot question**."

New refs tend to **pivot back**:

> "That's the third time today I've warned you."

> "Yeah, last game a team was complaining about the same thing."

> "I didn't see it, so I can't do anything about it."

Social Refs try and pivot to the future:

> "Who should I watch?"

> "Can you help me going forward?"

> "I will keep an eye on it for you!"

> "I will check with the other ref when I get a moment."

**Question #8 in your Script Sheet**: What future pivot will you use when players are complaining you missed something?

**SCRIPT SHEET**

Once you understand that pivots help break bad momentum, you can add more of them to your system.

New refs try to defuse a situation by talking to everyone at once, which has no impact, but is human nature when it comes to confrontation: Give a general announcement and hope the specific offenders change their bad ways.

You work at a company and two employees keep parking in the wrong spots and messing up the whole system for everyone. The company naturally sends out an office wide memo, asking EVERYONE to "remember" the parking policies.

Just get in front of the two people who are doing things wrong, and ask for their help!

> **Problem:** Players are doing something and you are trying to get them to stop.

**Beginner Brain Solution:** *"Hey everybody, keep it down/ knock it off/cut it out!!"*

**Ref Brain Pivot:** Specifically ask someone for help.

*"Captains, **I need your help**. There is way too much trash talking going on this game. I don't want the fun to get ruined and have to start throwing penalties every play. Can you help me out?"*

Go to specific players, captains, and coaches and DIRECTLY ask for help.

If all your warnings and requests are still being ignored, don't hesitate to use the simplest defuser:

**KEY CONCEPT**

**When things are heading in the wrong direction, stop the game and "send the meal back."**

Surely you have had a restaurant mess up your order at least once. Maybe you asked for no mayo, maybe you asked for the dressing on the side, maybe you ordered a different dish entirely.

You asked for your meal a certain way, and it did not go the way you asked. Are you going to say something when things are off? Or will you just ignore it and say, *"It doesn't matter,"* and "go with the flow".

Beginning refs often lack confidence to stop a game and "send the meal back"; they can't handle the potential awkwardness and anger. So problems keep getting worse until they eventually ruin the game.

Social Refs send the meal back—they pause the action with an official's timeout or a ref huddle—to stop bad momentum.

Want to practice confidence? Send the wrong food back. Step up for a friend or family member afraid to cause a problem at a restaurant. On the field, stop the game for an officials timeout, or to directly ask players for help.

In the Stabilize Phase, you need to feel comfortable sending a meal back and breaking bad momentum. It could be double-checking game info, huddling with your fellow refs, letting someone fix their gear, or just cooling things down. Sometimes a game-stopper can be the best pivot in your toolbox.

## Disarm and Defuse

Three more ways Social Refs defuse tension are: **compliments**, **escape hatches**, and **humor**.

**Compliments** "camouflage" bad news that players will instantly dislike.

The runner was out at 3$^{rd}$, but they *did* drive in a run on the play. The player still got the first down, or still retains possession. These small pivots have a surprisingly good track record of changing a player's focus from complaining about a call to being proud of an accomplishment.

> *"Great sack, but you were so fast that you were offsides, so we will go plus 5 and replay the down."*

> *"Wow, great location, now just slow the pitch down a little bit."*

Telling rec players they are "*too strong*," "*too fast*," or "*too good*" may sound silly, but it actually works because **everyone likes a compliment**. Notice in this case—unlike with the Historical Voice—we use "YOU" directly when delivering a nice compliment.

**KEY CONCEPT** **Be direct with "YOU" and "YOUR" when giving good news and compliments; be detached with the historical voice when assigning blame for penalties and fouls because they feel like criticism.**

Giving players an **escape hatch** means removing blame from the situation.

Many times when a player is arguing a call, they are pushing back because they need you to understand and acknowledge one simple idea: ***"I didn't do it on purpose."***

In some cases you can **pre-defuse** conflict by removing blame:

> *"You didn't mean to do it, but looked like that elbow came up and got the defender."*

The more aggressive contact on a call, the more a "pre-defuser" can help.

Accusing someone of elbowing, pushing, or shoving someone else is normally an auto-escalator. Don't be surprised if they defend themselves and their "honor" until the end of time. Giving them an escape hatch is a much better way to pre-defuse a situation.

Remember Hanlon's Razor, and *assume people are trying their best*. No one means to hurt someone, commit a huge penalty, or break a rule. Try and give them an escape hatch when you call them out on their mistakes.

**Humor** can be the most powerful defuser, provided that 1) it's not mean or sarcastic, 2) you're actually funny, and 3) the jokes are about YOU and your mistakes.

**As a ref, humor always works best when used for defense, never to go on offense.**

KEY CONCEPT

Most great Social Refs are able to "**own insults**" and respond to them with comedy instead of anger.

*"Gawd, ref you really suck at this!"*
**"I know right, I can't believe they let me work here."**

DEFUSER

*"That's the worst friggin' call of the day!"*
**"Don't worry, the day isn't over yet!"**

The right joke and a smile can be one of the best ways to disarm and calm down a situation. Just pick your spots and don't overdo it. Responding to a legitimate question with a joke, or making jokes after every play, will annoy many players and make things worse.

A joke doesn't need to be amazing, sometimes the lamest "Dad Joke" can be a way to "practice confidence" and break bad momentum:

> *"It's a dentists favorite time of the game; 2:30 on the clock and running."*

. . .Think about it for a second. . .

For **Question #9 in your Script Sheet:** What's your go-to defuse joke going to be?

**SCRIPT SHEET**

Roll out your humor defense slowly and carefully, and realize it can be one of the most effective ways to defuse tension and attacks directed at YOU.

# The Mega-Gift Defuser

We saved one of the best defusers for last:

**Take your game info and gift it to players.**

Who doesn't like getting a gift?

The best Social Refs *gift* game info to players, instead of just yelling it out loud.

> *"Hey batter, you got 1 out here."*
>
> *"QB, you have 2nd down and short cone to go."*
>
> *"Blue team, 2 minute warning—you still have 2 timeouts left for the game."*

The response will almost always be positive, just like with any gift or favor. People usually respond with "**thank you**"!

Experiment with this idea next time you are at the field. Walk through all the different ways you can try gifting info to coaches or players:

*"1 away."*

*"1 away, Batter."*

*"Batter, you have 1 away here."*

*"Batter, **I have 1 away for you**."*

Like a Camouflage Compliment, we are direct and use "YOU" when gifting info:

*"QB, **YOU** have 23 seconds, two timeouts, and **YOUR** clock is stopped."*

**Be specific and direct with compliments, praise, and gifting info.**

Rookie Refs **yell**.

Regular Refs **tell**.

Social Refs **gift**.

Gifting info generates connection, and lots of thank you's:

*Thanks, sir! Thanks, Ump! Got it, thanks!* Or even just that knowing nod from Morgan Freeman in *Shawshank*.

It's never a bad idea to collect as many "thank you's" as you can, because it's pretty hard for someone to be super pissed at you, when they are saying thank you all the time.

There are literally hundreds of ways you can generate thank you's, from brushing off a plate, to grabbing a ball or a bat for a player. It's just one more way to climb down off the pedestal. Do tiny favors for teams that other refs or umps might think are beneath them, to grow your credibility bank and collect thank you's that can be cashed in later when CAP shows up.

You can also use info gifts to break momentum with a player who is really upset.

I recently reffed a flag football game where the better team—winning the whole game—gave up a wide open TD pass with less than a minute left. I could see the captain/QB clenching his fists, looking to the sky, just steaming.

Some refs think, *"not my problem"*. Great Social Refs see an opportunity to change the future. I simply told him:

> *"Hey Mr. QB—no matter what happens on this extra point, you will have 25 seconds and two timeouts when you get the ball back."*

His attitude changed instantly because I distracted him from focusing on a terrible play, and instead "gifted" him the 25 seconds they still had left.

I basically told him: ***The game isn't over yet; you still have a chance.***"

Basic game info can be a really simple way to break bad momentum. Don't re-argue old calls with upset players—try gifting them new info instead.

Try wrapping your game info up as a gift, and see if you can collect more thank you's for your credibility bank.

## DEFUSER TOOLBOX RECAP

### General Tools

- Historical Voice
- Perspective Switch: What you saw vs. What they did
- Field Talk

### Stop and Squash

- Killer Comebacks
- Fake Defusers
- YES-NO Loop Responses
- Over-Explaining Calls
- Re-enactments
- Singling out/Pointing out Players
- Shaking Your Head No

### Listen and Agree

- Agree with a Smaller Part (person, not the call)
- Find 1 Good Thing
- Agree with Yourself (Face Cue)

### Pivot or Pause

- Timing Pivot (Let's talk about this more at the next break)
- "Watch For" Future Pivot
- Ask for Help
- Send the Meal Back
- Ref Huddle

### Disarm and Defuse

- Camouflage Compliment
- Humor (as defense)
- Escape Hatch
- Gift Info
- Collect Thank You's
- Smile!

## PHASE 4 RECAP

Learning to defuse CAP can change your whole career, but it begins with changing your instincts on conflict, insults, and comebacks.

Great refs have tough calls, and bad calls, but they always move through them. They take the tougher path and defuse conflict rather than ignoring it and hoping it goes away. They acknowledge, pivot, and defuse. They let people vent, give their perspective, and keep things moving. They don't get stuck in the quicksand of endless debates and conflict.

**KEY IDEAS**

- When trying to defuse, first don't add gas to the fire. Watch out for Fake Defusers, like telling someone to "*take a breath*" or "*calm down*". Your Beginner Brain loves these responses, but they just make situations worse.

- Fight against the "**Killer Comeback**": saying the easy thing that feels good in a moment of conflict.

- Responding to a player by simply ignoring, or responding with the opposite of what they just said (YES-NO) are both escalators.

- Reverse Beginner Brain instincts of falling into negative communication patterns (telling someone what DID NOT happen), and bringing complicated Classroom Talk to the field.

- Avoid the instinct to keep explaining a decision or call— it normally makes things worse. Re-enacting a play ALWAYS makes things worse. Squash that bug.

- Directly telling someone "this is what you did" is another escalator. Try using the **Historical Voice** instead to emphasize what you saw from your perspective.

- Don't build your communication system around a few Bad Apples, and be aware of situations where teams will turn quick and make you the story of the game.

- Think through the 1 or 2 player profiles who rile you up the most, give them a nickname, and have a plan when you encounter them on the field.

- When it feels like no one is listening, try specifically "asking for help" instead of begging and repeating requests multiple times to everyone.

- All defusion really comes down to listening, pivoting, and disarming. Use the starting toolbox ideas while you develop and practice your own defuser tools.

- Gift game info to your players proactively. You will collect thank you's, change momentum, and connect better with the game.

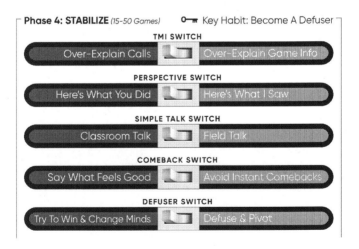

**Phase 4: STABILIZE** *(15-50 Games)*    ⊶ Key Habit: Become A Defuser

TMI SWITCH
Over-Explain Calls    Over-Explain Game Info

PERSPECTIVE SWITCH
Here's What You Did    Here's What I Saw

SIMPLE TALK SWITCH
Classroom Talk    Field Talk

COMEBACK SWITCH
Say What Feels Good    Avoid Instant Comebacks

DEFUSER SWITCH
Try To Win & Change Minds    Defuse & Pivot

## Practice

Practice confidence by finding game stopper situations in your everyday life, like at a restaurant. Don't be a jerk to waiters, but notice how often people shy away from "sending the meal back," and try helping them out.

Find examples of general warnings to everyone that really should be directed to a particular person.

Try out some corny "Dad Jokes" and get comfortable with general jokes to deal with a tense mood, and defensive jokes (own the insult) when you are under attack.

Gift out normal info in your day to day interactions:"*Leaving in 5 minutes!*" vs. "*You have 5 more minutes until you need to be in the car.*"

Instead of demanding things from friends and family over and over again, try "asking for help".

## PHASE 5: DRIVE (50+ GAMES)

# KEY HABIT: BE PROACTIVE, CHANGE THE FUTURE

All of the key habits we have discussed deal with the big idea of **engagement**:

- · How you relate to players

- · How you see the game

- · How you handle game info and the scoreboard

- · How you handle conflict and confusion

Will you ref big or small? Will you defuse conflict or escalate it? Will you own the scoreboard, or treat it like a chore? Will you build your own Script Sheet, or just "fake it till you make it" as issues come up?

Building the key habits of climbing down off the pedestal, seeing the Third Game, becoming the scoreboard, and defusing CAP give you the chance to free your brain to take another step in the Social Ref journey. We call this the Drive Phase, and it normally starts around your 50th game. That's when you decide whether you will continue on as a normal ref, or become a great Social Ref.

The Drive Phase is defined by our 5th Key Habit:

**Becoming a Proactive Ref who can *change the future*.**

**Proactive refs default towards action**. In this phase, they decide what kind of ref profile they will have, and what kind of philosophy they will form. They also master the idea of **Game Control**—being fully engaged in the game to the point where they can change the future for the better, and create more fun for players

# Proactive Reffing: Hats Off to You!

Doug plays flag football regularly on Sunday afternoons. He plays with work friends, and his company even pays part of the league fee (smart move). He isn't very good, and rarely gets the ball thrown to him, but he enjoys the competition and the exercise. He dreams of catching a TD in front of his boss.

You are going to destroy Doug's dream. A defender will slip and fall down in the end zone, leaving Doug *wide* open, and his boss—playing

QB—will throw a perfect pass that Doug will catch for a touchdown. And you will waive off Doug's touchdown because he was an "ineligible receiver," smashing his dreams into 100 pieces on the rocks of history—just by doing your job correctly as a *regular ref.*

You have seen an "ineligible receiver" call on TV before: a ref first throws their hat (and pats the top of their head) to show a player is "ineligible" after running out of the back of the end zone. If the player comes back in and catches the ball, it's a penalty and no TD.

Flag football leagues have this rule, too, and Doug was ineligible because players seldom watch their feet and the back line of the end zone; they are busy looking back at the QB. They *definitely* aren't looking down for hats.

Social Refs default to info, action, and being **proactive**:

> *"Hey boss, you keep running out of the back of the end zone—that's why I'm throwing my hat. I don't want to take away a big touchdown catch later, so watch that back yellow line for me, okay?"*

This is your "change the future" moment with Doug: by taking ten seconds to help him out **before there's even a problem**, you won't have to throw your hat as much in the first place, let alone wreck his dream with a "hat" call. You have *changed* the future.

Now Doug is thanking you instead of living out the rest of his days as a bitter, dreamless husk of a man, roaming the streets begging for change, and crying himself to sleep at night on a dirty, tear-stained, pillow.

More importantly, Doug sees you as a teacher and helper.

You can know all the rules, signals, and fouls to assess, but the difference between ordinary refs and the best Social Refs is always in **proactive communication**.

Don't forget the simplest start: **TRY to help!**

I've seen refs get downright angry and resentful at players who run out of the end zone, for *making them* throw their

**SIMPLE START**

hat. Maybe they could avoid all that anger by talking directly to the players first!

If you never teach and coach why you throw your hat, and TRY asking for help, you will just end up always throwing your hat.

You will crush Danielle's dream in softball: she will be so excited that she hit a clutch double, she will over-run second base, and get called out in the bottom of the 7th. You saw her over-run second base earlier after she had walked, but you didn't say anything. You hoped it wouldn't happen again, but it did.

Remembering is not a system for information. Hope is not a system for game control.

Dave will be in his kickball championship with his dream coming into focus—he can't remember ever winning anything this big *in his life*. He is so fired up that he slides head first into 3rd base, and you HAVE to call him out because head-first slides are an automatic out in your league. You noticed Dave almost slide head-first before, but he caught himself at the last possible second and it didn't impact the play, so you just moved along.

I've seen lots of Doug moments over the years. Watching someone feel bad because they drop a catch is no fun, but it's part of playing sports. Watching the joy and excitement drain out of someone's face *because you have to take something away from them* over a rule that you **could** have taught or helped with. . . that's a reason to become a better communicator.

**Sometimes your best call will be a simple warning.**

Default to action, teaching, helping, quick tips at the right time (before someone messes up) and taking ownership of your field and your game.

You can't fix everything and solve every problem, but you CAN help players and impact the "fun" more than you think. .

A Social Ref is ALWAYS proactive because they can change the future, and protect Doug's touchdown dream.

# Warnings and Lessons

*"Nice work, Brian!"* I say to a new ref who is about 70 games into his career. *"That's the best call you will make all day!"*

Brian's "big call"? He stopped the game and whistled the play dead because two little kids had walked into the end zone to say hi to their Dad on defense *seconds* before the snap

A warning, a game stopper, or a quick lesson may be the most important "call" you make all game.

You're on the job to make rulings and calls (The Ref Slice), but you are *also* there to make decisions and judgments that might not even revolve around a play (League Ops Slice/Field and Gear Slice).

**FIELD & GEAR MANAGER**

*Is this field safe to play on?*

*Is it raining too hard?*

*Is that a legal bat?*

*Is that dude wearing steel toe boots/metal cleats?*

*Is that other dude not wearing shoes at all?*

*There is a lady walking through left field with a kayak over her shoulder and a kid. What should I do now?*

[Someday when we meet up. . . ask about the riddle of the Kayak Story.]

You can only make these judgments once you decide to be more than a regular "**robot ref**": someone who just calls balls and strikes, safe and out, completions and out of bounds, and collects their check. . .

if there even is a paycheck. You do enough to move the game along, no more, and no less.

When you decide you want to be a proactive ref—and change the future—all the Doug opportunities that are never in the rule book or training sessions, will start to appear.

You need the confidence to pause a game, to start a conversation, and to sometimes tackle tough ideas head on, with a **warning**.

New refs see warnings as a drag, and deliver them like a scolding parent (auto-escalator).

Warnings can build your credibility and engagement—to the point that players will welcome the help and say "thank you"—*if* you get out of the Beginner Brain mindset that a warning always has to be "bad".

WARNING SWITCH

Negative & Scolding  |  Opportunity To Teach, Connect

Warnings are most effective when they are **specific, personal, and repetitive**.

New refs try to warn **everyone at once**.

A new player throws their bat up against the fence after a hit, almost smacking the umpire in the face. *"WATCH THE BAT!"* the ump yells at no one in particular while walking back to home plate. The runner is now on 1st, chatting with the first baseman, not even listening.

This always reminds me of the legendary Chris Farley as the bus driver in *Billy Madison*, screaming out *"NO YELLING ON THE BUS!"* to everyone—and no one. He is ignored, and quickly and awkwardly sits back down.

**Warnings should be personalized to players, coaches, or captains.**

When someone throws a bat really bad, I jog over to 1st base and have a 1-on-1 talk with them:

> *"Hey batter, I need your help with throwing the bat—it*

*bounced off the fence pretty hard there. Try dropping it next time."*

90% of the time, they respond with some form of *"Oh my gosh, I'm sorry, **I didn't even realize**."*

Next time the batter is up, instead of hoping they remember our chat at 1<sup>st</sup> base; I give them another proactive rep:

*"Batter, keep an eye on that bat for me."*

Just like game info, you might need to 3-rep your warnings before they can have any impact.

Sometimes it works, sometimes it doesn't. Nothing works every time. You still need an attitude that says, "I can change the future and make this better," rather than one that says, "I just hope bad things don't happen". If that attitude comes from avoiding a bat to the shin (trust me; it hurts), then that's fine too.

**Simple Start:** Practice warnings and proactive reffing with new players first. Co-ed and youth leagues always have new players and subs every week, well beyond week 1. If you are new to warnings, start with people that are new; they normally stick out pretty fast.

Goofy sports like kickball and dodgeball seem to bring out even more of these new players, as captains grab friends or co-workers 15 minutes before game time.

**Ref Myth:** Veteran teams and coaches will give me the biggest problems.

**Ref Truth:** Veteran teams may complain the most about specific rules or give refs a hard time, but **new players are always the most dangerous** because they have no idea what they are doing.

They always seem to force action just by being new. They don't know where to run. They don't know how to tackle. They stand on top of bases, including home plate. They don't know the rules, and a lot of times, they don't know how to control their own body.

Start practicing your warnings and quick lessons on new players. You might even start to build out a mini-speech to add to your growing Script-Sheet. For example, every time I have a new catcher, I always go over three quick points with a Universal "New Catcher" Habit.

This requires a simple proactive step. Don't forget to ASK, *"Howdy, have you ever played catcher before?"*

**SCRIPT SHEET**

**Question #10 on your Script-Sheet:** What are your proactive warnings and quick lessons for new players in your sport?

# Three Ways to "Have Their Back"

To engage with players proactively, use the 3 H's:

**THE THREE Hs**

*Hear Them*
*Help Them*
*Have Their Back*

We have learned to avoid dismissive responses and body cues when hearing players, and we have learned that warnings and quick teaching lessons are the best way to help them.

So let's look at three ways to "have their back."

## Keep the Call

I used to play a lot of blackjack; even read a book or two. The books all tell you that 16 is the most common hand you will lose with; a dealer will often beat it outright, or you will "bust" trying to make a better hand. The books also tell you that if the dealer has 10 showing and you have 16, you still *have* to hit—even though this is the **#1 situation you will lose in**—because doing nothing will cause you to lose even more money over time. Beginner blackjack players will hesitate to act in this spot, even when they know exactly what they're supposed to do—sound familiar?

New refs "**stand on 16**" a lot: they wait, they resist action because it might "hurt," they hope for good outcomes even when the math tells them they need to act instead. Proactive refs might not be right every single time, but they default to action to change the future.

One reason I've always appreciated flag football as a place to start your career is that you can call a penalty, and then decide to pick it up. There have been many times where I've thrown a flag, had a quick ref huddle, and waived it off.

You *could* decide to AVOID making a call altogether, because you will just end up waving it off. A receiver in the end zone catches a TD pass while the defender lands on their shoulders for an easy Pass Interference call. Why still make the call? *The receiver caught the pass for a TD!*

Default to action and **keep the call**. Make sure everyone sees you throw that flag. It will take you an extra 5 seconds to explain, "*We have Pass Interference on the defense. That penalty is declined and the TD is good*," but it's a huge part of game control.

The receiver knows you are engaged, and that you have their back.

Beginners that skip the call or penalty also fail to notice how that player reacts.

The receiver gets mauled in the end zone, doesn't see a flag, and feels nobody has their back:

> *"Well, if **that's** not a penalty, then next time I'm on defense, I will return the favor to that jerk who landed on me."*

And down your game goes into a spiral of bad momentum.

Let players know about infractions and fouls, even if they don't count, even if you will eventually take them back, or re-do the play.

*"Flag was pulled before the flag guard,"* tells everyone that you are on your game, you saw the pull, and you ALSO saw the flag guard.

> **"Watch that leg 1ˢᵗ base, if the runner was closer that could have been an obstruction for blocking the base."**

As you progress, you will have more opportunities to layer your communication like this, teaching and explaining while still being in control of your game. Don't miss opportunities to show everyone you saw action and are engaged, even if you don't make a call or end up taking one back.

## Step In + Step Up

Sometimes, in a blowout game, you can *feel* that a team is totally demoralized. There's no ruling or call to make, but as a Social Ref, you need to decide when you will step into a situation to defend a player or a team. You can always say something when teams run up the score, take extra bases, or just act like huge turds.

Really good softball teams can "pick on a fielder," hitting balls directly to the worst outfielder on a bad team. When you first get started, this should not be your focus. One hundred games in, it will still take some confidence, but you will know it when you see it. You can decide to step up and say something:

> **"I think you guys can stop hitting it at the right fielder now that you are up 18 runs."**

You might notice in soccer or basketball that the same "star" players keep getting fouled over and over again. Will you say something?

I recently watched my soccer friend Scott stop a game and call a foul while politely letting the defense know that it was the fourth foul of the game on a certain player, and the next one would be a Yellow Card. Surprisingly, that player was left alone for the rest of the match.

Sometimes players are just being bad sports: pulling flags and throwing them 5 yards away, or bending-but-not-breaking rules. In Underdog Kickball you can get someone out by tagging a base, tagging them with the ball, or throwing the ball at them and hitting them below the neck. You'd be surprised how often one player rears back and hurls the ball at another player two feet in front of them instead of taking the easy out.

This is an auto-escalator, and I will always say something.

### *"Totally unnecessary throw is good for the first out! Time called!"*

In softball or kickball, whenever the offense starts yelling "DROP IT" at fielders trying to make a play, or starts using "fake tags" at third base, I will always step in.

The same goes for insults or mean jokes. Sometimes a joke you think is actually pretty funny can spark a situation that will leave no one laughing.

In a men's football league years ago, people started making "yo mama" jokes in the 2nd half of a blowout game. Everyone laughed and thought they were funny at first; 20 minutes later, I was calling the game because of too much trash-talking, as one of the guys banged a metal pipe on the fence challenging everyone else to a fight.

Still not sure where he got the metal pipe from.

That story might be a crazy outlier, but I stepped in on jokes after that, even if they were funny. You never know how someone else can take a joke about their dear old mama.

I was reffing football last summer when a QB juked out a rusher, said, *"Get that sh\*t out of here!"* and sprinted down the field for a 20-yard gain.

The rusher didn't care, but that's still a spot to step in—maybe with a Camouflage Compliment and a warning:

> **"Hey QB, great run, but please, no more comments to the rusher like that."**

The QB first seemed shocked, asking, *"What did I do?"* At half-time he approached me: *"Yeah, I see what you were talking about. That's a good call."*

It wasn't actually a call at all, just a compliment layered with a request, letting him know that I heard the trash talk.

**When in doubt, don't assume. . . let them know you heard it, and saw it.**

**KEY CONCEPT**

Stepping in on bad conduct or poor sportsmanship may even feel like the wrong move at first (*"What's the matter ump, I was just joking"*), but many times, teams will let you know after the game that they saw it and appreciated your effort.

If you see good sportsmanship, or a great play, please compliment that, too. When you see a player slowing up to avoid a collision, or a player admits they were out because you had no angle on the play, thank them for their help. Find the good things you want others to see and copy.

Default to action. Step in when things feel wrong. Speak up and highlight when things are right. Let players know you have their back.

## Guard Their Time

There will *always* be things that slow your game down: injuries, gear problems, late refs, weather, or maybe a terrible accident that shuts down the highway. A shift that starts on time can slip very quickly.

If you really want to have a team's back, "guard their time".

A game might not feel fair if all the calls go against you, even if you deserved them.

**A game ALWAYS feels unfair when you didn't get your full time.**

KEY CONCEPT

There are two kinds of time situations: a HARD CAP and a SOFT CAP.

Some games have a running clock, while other leagues have an EITHER/OR setup, e.g. *"7 Innings or 1 hour. . . whichever comes first."*

Quickly identify if you are in a hard cap or soft cap situation during your shift. A hard cap means your league runs from 7-10PM and at 10PM, it's "game over": the lights turn off, another group has the field, or an attendant comes in to start yelling. Things just stop.

A soft cap situation means your league is scheduled for a certain time, but if you go over, nothing crazy happens. Your league runs from 12-6PM on a Sunday, but if the last game goes until 6:15 and you want to be awesome, you could stay and finish like a hero.

Answer two big questions:

***Do you know how to correctly "cut time"?*** Many refs think the way to cut time is to just shorten the game, but you can do better than that. Every sport has a way to shave a few minutes here and there. You can limit warm-up pitches between innings. You can shave a 5-minute break or halftime to 2 minutes. Figure out the best way to make up time when you are behind, because you *will* fall behind.

***Can you avoid an "info surprise"?*** These crop up in clock situations where a ref fails to announce the scoreboard info or the game clock enough. They abruptly call "half" as players are getting ready for the next play. They announce that the 5th inning will be the last inning. . . *during* the 5th inning. Ending a half or game early and without warning is the ultimate info surprise.

If you need to call a game short, or call the 5th inning the last inning, be proactive and make it clear and obvious to everyone well before the end. **Tell teams before the game even starts that you are running behind, and ask for their help.** You will be amazed at how teams hustle when you involve them in protecting their own time. Guarding time earns players respect, because it's such a central part of teams feeling like they got a fair chance and a full game.

# Special Sauce & Extra Sauce

If you want to make potential problems easier for players to digest, add some special sauce.

Special sauce is the unique delivery that refs start to develop around 50-60 games: getting away from a monotone delivery, and getting their Announcers Voice to feel more laid back and conversational, even when game info is urgent and important.

Social Refs tend to get more "slangy" with their delivery as they develop. They drop the "*Yes, sir*" from the customer service trap, and end up with more "*Yeah, I got you*" and "*Boy, I hear that.*" Often the more conversational your announcements, the more people will actually hear you.

Flight attendants now add jokes to the pre-flight safety announce-ments because people have heard them so many times they tune it out—that's their "special sauce".

A new ref yells OUT at the top of their lungs on a close play at 1$^{st}$ base. A Social Ref will calmly say, "*Ooouuuuuttttt at one, just got em*" in a way that translates to,"*Man, that's a bummer.*" They nod their head in a way that makes the player feel like they understand what just happened, and makes the call more believable.

Flip it around for a crazy kickball play where the ball bounces three times and then hits the runner on the foot: a "*GOT 'EM on the foot!!*" in a "special sauce" voice sounds amazed and elevates as the play ends.

In both cases the special sauce helps sell the call.

We call the empathetic call a "Droopy Call," and the excited call a

"Chuckle Call." They are pretty difficult to describe in print, but jump over to www.socialref.net/sauce for examples of special sauce calls like these that you can start using in the Drive Phase.

Don't worry about this kind of stuff in your first 15 games, but closing in on your first 100, your Ref Brain will naturally start to add some flavor to close and repetitive calls.

Your special sauce makes food the players may not like easier to swallow, because it again shows engagement through communication.

Adding some *extra* sauce has two components: can you add more info to help pre-defuse a call, and can you watch out for missing words that can make all the difference?

Remember—after the call we don't want to get stuck in an endless explanation loop. Proactively adding extra sauce to the call itself can cut down on the amount of pushback and conflict you get from players.

Sprinkle in some extra sauce with your communication sequences:

### *"Incomplete"* vs. *"Incomplete–foot was on the line."*

How about a coin-flip call at 1ˢᵗ base:

### *"SAFE!"* vs. *"SAFE at 1!"* vs. *"Safe at 1—foot was off the bag!"*

This is the same call, just with some added sauce. You address the instant reaction and conflict—*WHY ARE THEY SAFE?*—inside of the call (knowing that no one except you and Neo were watching the foot), instead of waiting for the question or argument after the call.

You can call:

### *"Ball! 1–0"* vs. *"Ball Outside! 1–0"* vs. *"Ball just a bit outside, brings up 1–0."*

You can bark out, "BALL" really loudly, but when you add the extra sauce of *"just a bit outside"*, it makes your communication more conversational and easier to accept and understand.

You can even add sauce when your whistle "talks" for you.

Quick chirps on a whistle are good for stopping play, killing action, and getting peoples' attention. Long bursts are good for starting play, and saying something was achieved, like a catch or a score.

If a player gets their flag pulled just short of the goal-line, but thinks they scored, you better believe I am running towards the spot, pointing at the spot and "chirping" my whistle multiple times to emphasize the player was down.

The second reason to add extra sauce info is that sometimes the power of a few "**missing words**" can prevent future conflict and confusion.

There are many ways to announce the game clock:

> *28 seconds!*
>
> *28 seconds left, Red Team!*
>
> *28 seconds in the game!*

New refs sometimes forget the most important extra sauce:

> *28 seconds on the clock AND RUNNING!*

Half the players on the field will think it's 28 seconds and stopped, half will think it's running. No one remembers the rule of whether the clock runs in the moment, so just give them the extra sauce!

The power of a couple of missing words shows up over and over in many situations.

Take timeouts. See how we can layer some extra sauce:

> *Timeout called!*
>
> *Timeout called: Blue!*
>
> *Timeout called: Blue, that's your first timeout!*
>
> *Timeout called: Blue, that's your first timeout—you have two left!*
>
> *Timeout called:, Blue, that's your first—you have two left*

### FOR THE GAME!

Have I had games end with teams complaining about how many timeouts they used?

You bet your BBQ sauce! Add the extra info.

Extra sauce can also help with YES–YES arguments: situations where a ref and player are arguing and they are both right!

> **"Safe!"**
>
> *"No way! The ball got there before the runner!"*
>
> **"Yes, the runner is still safe."**

This comes up a lot in The Trio when the force is off at a base, and a fielder—probably new—doesn't understand that they have to tag the runner for an out. The solution is to add more sauce:

> *"Safe at 2—no tag!"*
>
> *"No way! The ball beat the runner!"*
>
> **"Yes, but force is off so you need to tag the runner."**
>
> *"Ohhhhhhh. . .  cool. . .  what's a force?"*

This extra sauce of *"no tag"* is a great example of a **teach and tell** moment: a spot where you can teach and announce the game at the same time.

In college baseball, the umps may have to deal with a ton of crap, but they don't have to teach people that you can over-run 1st base, but never over-run second or third. They never have to explain "tag-ups" and "sac flies" and staying on base when the ball is hit in the air with less than 2 outs. In your rec league, these are situations where you can be proactive and change the future.

Take a normal announcement you would make over and over again for a football extra point attempt:

> **"Offense, going for 2 here!"**

Now add some **teach and tell** extra sauce.

*"Offense is going for a 2 pointer; **as always, that's returnable for 2 points.**"*

Teach and tells can be incredibly powerful—especially for all the new players at your leagues—but only if you add some extra sauce to repetitive game info and sequences.

Normal refs get the call out of the way quick to prepare for conflict. Social Refs add their own special flavor, and then add extra sauce, to minimize confusion and conflict.

Which path will you choose?

Try the one with extra mustard.

# Own the Field

Part of "game control" is owning your field. Social Refs take responsibility for the field or court they are working, even when they have nothing to do with a problem.

Step #1 in owning the field: **Be early**.

Refs who consistently show up 20 minutes early always seem to work out. Refs that are always "stuck in traffic," or putting their uniform on as they walk in the stadium—*amazingly*, also seem to struggle with becoming the scoreboard and being engaged in the game.

When you show up early, you can deal with some crazy things that can easily derail your league:

> There are no bases on the field.
>
> Someone left a bunch of folding chairs and tables on your field.
>
> There is broken glass on the field.

The lights aren't turning on.

A group thinks they have the field reserved instead of you.

All of these situations can come up in a given day. It's hard to prevent them, especially if you are using public parks and sharing space, but it is easier to deal with them when you show up early.

**FIELD & GEAR MANAGER**

You can walk the field and notice a sprinkler head, or a pothole, or a wobbly base. You notice that a line is faded and that you should put down discs or cones to reinforce it. Maybe that line only comes into play once your whole shift, but you will be glad you showed up 5 minutes earlier and owned your field.

Sometimes fields have spots where a line doesn't exist at all. We call these "naked lines," and they can create big problems for refs. In our flag football league, the corners of our end zones will have naked lines, and when the controversial TD catch/call happens in the back corner, new refs who don't show up early and own the field will blame the lines for their indecision.

*"What can I do? There wasn't a line to use. . . "*

*Naked Lines in the End Zone*                    *Dressed Lines with Discs*

I know what you could do. . . show up 5 minutes earlier and put down some discs.

Beginners say, *"Screw that, I'm here to ref, not put down cones."*

Great Social Refs know the one time they have a close call, they will be glad they owned the field and put down those discs. Naked lines show up everywhere: football, kickball, dodgeball, softball. Some turf fields have too many lines and need some cones/discs for clarity.

Social Refs show up early, own the field, and notice when something is off. They notice when a player brings a bike, a bag, *a baby stroller* too close to the sideline. They notice when someone's Bluetooth speaker is too loud, with music full of curse words, and parents or fans are shooting nervous looks at each other. They notice that backpack or metal water bottle just waiting to get stepped on.

*Two of the biggest villains. . . the METAL water bottle on the sideline and the backpack too close to the end zone line.*

When you are rushed and late, everything gets foggy. You don't notice simple things with your field, and with the players:

> A team that swapped their ball in for your league game ball.
>
> A team with a couple of players that are clearly playing the sport for the first time.
>
> A team trying to pick up a sub for the playoffs.
>
> A doofus who decided to wear metal cleats to a rec sports league.

Sometimes the best call you make is noticing your field and talking to the players before your game even starts. Tell that guy to change his shoes before the game starts, instead of after an injury in the 4th inning. Tell a parent to move the baby stroller further back.

When a preventable problem crops up later in the game, will you be mad at them, or will you look at yourself and your system?

If you want to blame players for arguing, making mistakes, and doing silly things like putting their bike right next to the field, you will never run out of people to blame in a rec league.

Great refs don't blame the players, or make excuses—they get better. . . even with the weather!

The shift that gives me the least amount of problems and CAP is always **the one where I am pushing puddles off the field an hour before the game starts**. When both teams show up, they realize the game wouldn't even be happening if the ump wasn't also owning the field.

If you care about the field, you care about the game, and players notice.

## Split the Field

Part of owning the field is simply moving around to spots that most refs don't get to. Many refs end up "stuck" in certain parts of the field at the end of plays. Umps in the Trio end up stuck behind home plate. Refs for football end up stuck on the sidelines. Some basketball refs as the "trail official" always seem stuck at half court, getting ready for the play to go the other way. Show players that you will meet them where they are, and that you will follow the game by moving towards the action.

Draw a line from 3$^{rd}$ base, through the pitching rubber, and then through 1$^{st}$ base. How many plays will finish up on the other side of that line? Will you be there to see them?

If you are on a football field, draw a small rectangle inside of the larger rectangle of your field. How many times will you end up in the smaller rectangle—to talk to players, give warnings, or just make a good spot?

Proactive refs split the field. They never have to worry about shouting or yelling warnings because they always seem to end up next to the person they want to talk with—maybe a pitcher or the QB. Face-to-face communication is always better for game control than shouting or whistling across the field to get someone's attention.

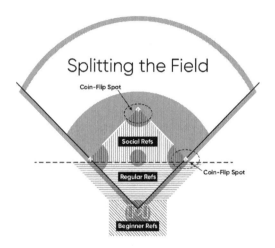

If you never get out from behind home plate, you can't see a wobbly base at 1<sup>st</sup> or 3<sup>rd</sup>. You can't see if there is literally something on your field.

Move and split the field, and you will be able to hear more, see more issues with gear, and be more engaged in the game.

Go where the action is to communicate with players and own the field.

### Finish Strong

You showed up early, owned the field, reffed a tough game and did a really good job.

Don't blow the ending by venting about the "silly" players **while they are still there on the field after the game**.

> *"That QB was so dumb! All he had to do was take a knee there and the game is over, but instead he throws a*

*INT??? Can you believe it?"*

Yup, I can. It has happened a ton of times, and will keep happening. It's rec sports. What I can't believe is that you are talking out loud with the QB only 15 feet away, looking over at us, still feeling bad about what happened.

**When you gossip, make fun, or even complain about the teams that just played, you are setting the stage for your next game with waiting teams and players that are *already watching you*.**

Finish your game the right way. There is a time and a place to vent about crazy pills and crazy plays with your fellow refs. Right after your game finishes is the wrong time and place. Finish your game strong. Make sure the two players who didn't like each other shake hands the right way. Double check your final score, and that you wrote down any info you needed. Wait until EVERYONE is gone before you "take off your uniform" and vent a little.

# Take the Arrows. . .

Sports bring out competition. Competition brings out passion, contact, ego, pride and misunderstanding. Sometimes there will be arrows flying across the field and you'll have to take one that wasn't even meant for you.

Trash-talking and fights never appear out of the blue. They always build over time. 90% of the time you have an ejection or a fight on your field, it's something YOU could have prevented earlier (the Accountability Switch). When you are not engaged in your game, and you are afraid to issue warnings and defuse situations, things build until they break.

Fights and ejections should be extremely rare, because they signify that something went really wrong.

Fights come from attention issues more than behavior issues. *Where were you on the field? What were you listening to? Were you stuck behind home plate when the first baseman and the runner started trading insults?*

Ejections come from a lack of proactivity. *Did you give warnings? Did you stop the game? Did you confront problems head on with specific Bad Apples, or just hope for them to go away?*

 **Only making the EASY calls can lead to some very HARD games.**

**KEY IDEA**

Defuse early by taking the arrows meant for others. Some refs will jump out of their shoes with a Killer Comeback if *they* are insulted, but will barely notice if one team is insulting or attacking another team.

A few ways to take the arrows:

**Always step in when people are arguing about the rules.**

In *every* sport, you will hear players accusing people on the other team of doing something wrong or breaking a rule.

> *"Hey, the rules say you can't do that!"*

 **If players are arguing about rules, and you are standing there watching, you are doing something wrong.**

**KEY CONCEPT**

Step in. Make a joke. Do *something* to take those arrows.

> *"Hey guys, this is what they pay me the big bucks for. Talk to me about the rules."*

**Step in between players who look like they want to cause trouble.**

Split up players who are "close-talking'" in other's faces, pointing at each other, and entering the *"you better hold me back"* dance.

Warnings are good up to a certain point, but in certain cases, you need more than just another warning.

I use the formula **Split, Separate, and Wait (SSW)**.

> **Split** the players and step in between them. I will literally split their physical space.

> **Separate** the closest person. "*Walk with me*," is always a good start.

> **Wait** until things cool down. Assess penalties or fouls if you need to.

**Be aware of outside conflict.**

In general, you don't want players talking to random people that wander on to your field. They can be rude and crude.

One day I watched a player get into it with a guy walking his dog on a softball field 10 minutes before the game.

> "*This isn't your f\*cking dog park, dude.*"

> "*Whoa. . . Let me handle this, please*," I said, stepping in quickly.

Players will defend their field, and they will defend their time being wasted by random spectators and strangers. Always step in between those situations—it's just another part of owning your field.

Rules arguments, trash-talking, taunting, complaints about the field/fans/spectators—take the arrows where you can. You have tough skin. You're a ref!

Being proactive means not only stepping into your calls, but stepping in front of common situations to take arrows that will ruin your game.

# Your Reffing Profile

*"Where some people have a self, most people have a void, because they are so busy PROJECTING themselves as this or that. This is again the curse of the ideal. **The curse is that you should not be what you are.**"*

— Bruce Lee, *Artist of Life*

Now you can drive towards your ref profile. What kind of role will you play? Listen to Bruce Lee and be who you are first.

If you aren't a natural jokester, don't turn into a comedian just because you start reffing.

If you aren't a bossy person—or a drill sergeant—don't pretend to be one at the field.

If you aren't a technician in life, why start over-reffing on the court?

The ref stripes will not transform you from Clark Kent into Superman. You're still *you*. *So who are you*?

Take a look at some of the most common profiles we have seen and think about where you belong:

**The Jester**: Always a smile, and always a joker. It's hard to ever pin the Jester down, even in the heat of the moment, because they turn everything into a joke. Veteran players normally love the Jester, but they can certainly rub new players, captains, and coaches the wrong way. Jesters are masters at defusion, and seldom get caught in arguments or debates, because they will wiggle out of tough situations with humor.

> **DIAGNOSIS**: *Sounds great! Everyone should just be a Jester, right?* Nope. Not everyone can pull it off. If you are not a natural comedian and you can't easily add humor to a tense situation,

don't go down this road; it will blow up in your face.

**The *Aww Shucks* Ref**: A cousin of the Jester, the Aww Shucks Ref defuses by owning every insult, criticism, and responsibility with a smile and laid-back nature. Their demeanor makes it seem like they are just getting the hang of things, or that they are an observer more than a judge. You will hear a lot of "*aww shucks*" comments when players complain about missed calls—things like, "*I will do better next time*". Smiles rule the day.

> **DIAGNOSIS**: Aww Shucks Refs do a great job at deflecting and defusing conflict—normally by embracing any kind of criticism— but they sometimes defuse at the cost of their own credibility. "*Aww shucks, I am just doing my best*" works well in some situations with some teams, but in the stressful moments of big games, the Aww Shucks Ref gets in trouble fast.

**Mr. Miyagi**: From the classic film, *The Karate Kid*, Mr. Miyagi is always trying to teach and coach every player, offering words of encouragement and compliments. Mr. Miyagi's are optimists at heart; every mistake can be coached or corrected. Sometimes they even hesitate to call a penalty, because "*the player didn't really mean to do that on purpose; they just need some help!*"

> **DIAGNOSIS**: Mr. Miyagi is loved by many players, but can also be accused of bias and favoritism, and become annoying to some players and fans who don't want advice and input on every play. Coaching and teaching is a valuable job of the Social Ref, but the timing and context of that coaching is always important. Keep in mind—**the worst time to give advice or a lesson is often right after someone just made a huge mistake.**

**The Ice Warrior**: Stone cold in looks, body language, and communication, the Ice Warrior Ref doesn't mince words—they barely say anything. It's a no-nonsense, just-the-facts approach to the game. A foul is a foul and a penalty is a penalty, and there is nothing more to say.

> **DIAGNOSIS**: Often highly precise on protocol and procedure, an Ice Warrior Ref thrives in pressure situations, but can sometimes over-ref when things are just normal. Sometimes

they look to make calls that just aren't necessary. Since they have no fans, their best friend is normally the rulebook. They often have to demand attention and respect, because their demeanor means most players see them as a judge, critic, or even an enemy.

**The Mayor of Refville**: The Mayor wants to know everyone's name, birthday, and favorite ice cream. They spend all of their free time shaking hands and kissing babies. They will often introduce themselves with their name and immediately ask you for yours, sometimes even joking with players by their first name during a game.

> **DIAGNOSIS**: The mayor is everyone's buddy, sometimes to a fault. They are "well-liked," but often grumbled about behind their back. They have the dynamic personality to be everyone's best friend, but those "friendships" often don't last after a big call that doesn't go someone's way. Trying to be every player's buddy and make everyone happy can get in the way of officiating a solid game.

**As much as you might try and pick one of these profiles, they normally pick you.**

No ref fits perfectly in any one box. Some refs try to assemble a hybrid with the best ideas from each profile. Are you an Aww Shucks/Jester? A Mayor who dabbles in the Iceman when someone pushes back on you?

Great Social refs weave in and out of several profiles on any given day. Maybe for a couple of new teams they are Mr. Miyagi; for a group of middle-of-the-road teams they take on a Aww Shucks flavor, and for the most competitive teams they become an Ice Warrior Ref with a sprinkling of Jester.

Choosing a profile *before* you start reffing is kind of like choosing a major on your first day of college. First, you have to go through the earlier phases, learn the habits, and go through some tough **Growth Games** that change who you are and how you think.

Once you have reached the Drive Phase, you can proactively decide if you need to take on a different profile for a certain game or setting. You don't need to stay stuck in one mode; try out several, or a combination of ideas that work for you. Just make sure—like Bruce Lee says—you aren't trying to force yourself to be someone other than who you really are inside.

## PHASE 5 RECAP

If you want to be a Social Ref for the long haul, believe that you can change the future.

If you are going to make mistakes, reffing proactively is the place to make them.

The bigger mistake is sliding back into being a spectator once you get comfortable.

The biggest mistake is knowing the game needs you to step up, and not even trying.

New refs are always watching, and waiting for the perfect moment to step in and step up.

Don't wait. Be proactive. Change the future.

**KEY IDEAS:**

· Social Refs believe that they can change the future, and default to action.

· Warnings can be better than calls or penalties. They don't need to be attacks; they can be opportunities to teach and build credibility.

· 3 proactive ways to show you have a players back: Keeping a call, guarding time, and stepping in.

· The three H's—*Hear me, Help me, Have my back*—are key to engagement with your teams and players.

- As you get more comfortable, layer extra information—your own special sauce—into your calls. This will help player understanding and keep them from ignoring info.

- To control your game, start by owning the field, owning the gear, and being early.

- Always take the arrows, even if conflict on the field is not directed towards you.

- Make sure as you drive towards your ref profile, you don't try and become someone different from who you really are.

**Phase 5: DRIVE & THRIVE** *(50 Games+)* ⚬—ᴡ Key Habit: Change The Future

PROACTIVE SWITCH

Wait & Watch ▸ Default To Action

WARNING SWITCH

Negative & Scolding ▸ Opportunity To Teach, Connect

ACCOUNTABILITY SWITCH

It's The Players ▸ It's My System

## Practice

Try "taking the arrows" in normal situations at work or around family.

Work on "being early" if you know that is not one of your strong suits.

In your Ref Journal, write down examples of when you changed the future in a game and no one even noticed.

Start using SSW and scripts with people who are angry with other players or fans.

## OVERTIME: KEEP PRACTICING

# OFF-FIELD PRACTICE

The best Social Refs make it look effortless.

**That is because they put so much effort into building their system when no one is watching**

It might look easy in the moment, because they are operating on habits and muscle memory. Those habits took a lot of work and practice to build.

You have switches to focus on, movement and sequences to try, scripts to develop, and some starter defuser tools.

Now what?

Practice, of course. Practice so much that announcing your game information becomes like breathing.

Practice so much that starting to defuse becomes like tying your shoe.

Practice so much that your instant reaction to conflict becomes a calm response from your Script-Sheet, as if you were brushing your teeth in the morning.

We talked about drilling in front of the mirror because we believe it works.

Have you tried it yet?

We talked about building a Script-Sheet, summarized in the back of this book. Have you built yours yet? Or did you read over that section and think, *"That's interesting, I have to remember to do that later."*

**At some point you will run out of "laters."**

Cam, one of the best Social Refs we have ever seen, seemed to pick things up "effortlessly." He must have been a natural. . . right? Was he just "born" to ref?

We took him out to lunch one day, and asked how he quickly got to be so good. His answer probably won't surprise you:

He told us a story about drilling all of the hand signals as he was walking across campus.

To Cam, an 8-minute walk to class could have been a chance to pull up his phone and hop on Facebook or Twitter. Instead it was 8 more minutes drilling the core communication sequence with signals, so they became like breathing when the games finally came around.

You might find this trait across many successful people in life—they always seem to attack the "**random 12 minutes**." Maybe an insane fitness person you know is always doing push-ups or handstands everywhere. Maybe a budding young entrepreneur sees a 12-minute car ride as an opportunity to listen to a business leader on audio book.

When I was younger, I can remember reading an article on one of my favorite basketball players in Sports Illustrated, Steve Nash. They talked about how insane he was at practicing his dribbling all the time in college. Take a guess how he practiced?

He would take a tennis ball, and dribble it. . . as he was walking across campus between classes.

Sound familiar?

After a while, you realize that your habits and systems are more important than the end goal. It's your system that will ultimately determine success whatever path you choose: basketball, reffing, gymnastics, sales or business. You get to decide.

Successful people attack that "random 10 minutes," that "8-minute walk to class," or that "12-minute car ride". Those minutes add up to a better CCS and game info, or dribbling better with your left hand, or developing a granny shot. Your system makes repetitive communication easier so you see more opportunities to be a proactive Social Ref.

Compare any two refs for 2 minutes. You might have thought at first we would judge them based on accuracy or rule book knowledge. I would judge them on how they announce the score. Give me the ref who has made announcing the score and game info an automatic habit. That's a ref who understands to get to the important stuff, like the big call, they need to nail the basic game info first to build credibility in the bank.

Love sports? Guess who else loved sports? Every single ref candidate who flamed out with Underdog over the last 18 years because they refused to build and use a communication system.

Loving sports is never enough.

Twelve minutes every weekday is an hour a week, and 50 hours a year. The difference between being okay and grinding through, versus being good or great is not in those 50 or 100 or 10,000 hours, but starts with those 12 minutes. Think about those 12 minutes next time you are in the car, sitting in a waiting room, watching Netflix before you go to sleep, or even walking across campus.

**Those 12 minutes are yours, if you claim them.**

There is no substitute for the right kind of practice: communication, defusion, humor, and information sequences, not just reading that dang rulebook over and over again.

# The Sandbox

In the software sense, a "sandbox" is a simulated setting where you can practice your ideas and skills and nothing bad happens if you mess up.

Pros find and use Sandboxes.

The biggest stars in comedy will play the smallest clubs—unannounced—to test out new material and get feedback.

Look to create those Sandboxes on your own.

Can you invite 8 of your friends to a park and say you will ref their game for free?

Can you ask your league if there are any pre-season games, open houses, clinics, or exhibition games you can ref?

Can you go to a local community center and see if they need volunteer refs? (They almost always do.)

Better yet:

Is there ever a situation where you have a forfeit at the actual leagues, but you can encourage the teams to still play and ask to be the head official?

I have taken refs actually working their first hour and said, *"You are the head line ref for this exhibition game."*

Do they mess up? Sure! But it's a Sandbox—if they mess up, literally next to nothing happens, except for a few embarrassing growth reps we get out of the way early. You can see a forfeit as a break, or a Sandbox.

You could also try **"downshifting a level"** to a league with less at stake to practice seeing the Third Game (middle school football in Minnesota was the Sandbox where I began learning how to ref).

If you're not confident enough to stop the game in a youth league, how are you going to do it in a high school or adult rec league game? If you can't warn a 12-year-old about blocking low, or grabbing a face mask, how are you going to talk to a 30-year-old player or a 50-year-old coach whose job might be on the line?

Youth leagues, local community centers, and organizations like the Special Olympics would probably love your help, no matter your skill level. I get Sandbox reps reffing my 7-year-old daughter's basketball league. After 10 games, I could see things I never noticed as a fan: where to move, how to signal change of possession, and how to protect a kid who sits down on the court to tie their shoes in the middle of a game. (That might also be your best call of the day.)

If you are struggling with the idea of Classroom Talk vs. Field Talk, go work a game with some elementary school kids. They will help you simplify your language pretty quickly, because big words and long winded explanations just get ignored. I'm pretty sure they haven't read the rulebook, but they have read *Green Eggs and Ham*.

Ask your league if they have any audio or video of past games that you can watch—a good ref Sandbox. If none exists, getting game video with smart phones and iPads and GoPros is easy. Sometimes players in the league will even post their own game footage to YouTube. Find a 5-or 10-minute clip online to practice your signals and game info.

Practice and drill when you can. Find Sandboxes to practice your calls, scripts, and communication. Maybe you need to create a Sandbox, or shift down a level to get started. Anyway you can, keep your eyes out for Sandboxes. They are likely all around, once you start looking for the opportunity.

# Recorders and Recordings

**SIMPLE START**

**Simple Start**: Record yourself reffing. Then listen to the recordings in your spare time.

There are a number of ways to do this: most smart phones allow you to record easily. Often, I will bring a small digital recorder with a "lapel mic" to games and record the audio to chop up and use in future videos.

Check in with your league and your supervisors to make sure this is okay, and have a good response if a player happens to notice that you are wearing a microphone.

Once you get past that initial weirdness—and any of your own nerves—you will see that recording yourself is great way to get better and be accountable.

Your brain can remember things quite differently than how they actually happened. Just as players can think, "*the ref screwed us*," it's always easier for a ref to blame a player for being mean or escalating a situation. When you listen to a recording and hear the fake defuser YOU used that started the problem. . . that is harder to wiggle out of.

I record most major meetings, speeches and presentations, catching ideas that might come out spontaneously, or accidentally. These can be nice additions to your system. (I first recognized that I was "gifting players info" when I heard a recording and noticed my Ref Brain doing it instinctively to collect thank you's.)

You can listen to your delivery and presentation on a recording. If your recorder is good enough, you can even hear the audience and note when a joke fell flat, or when you rushed a delivery, or when you kept over-explaining, or lost your way.

**PRACTICE**

Pros talk about "watching tape". A pro football team goes back and watches game footage on Monday, seeing what they did well, and what they messed up. If you are trying to become a better communicator, listen to the tape of your last shift. You will hear things on a second and third listen that you will never notice in live action. You can hear the escalators and Beginner Brain switches that still need work.

Recordings convey ultimate accountability. Great quarterbacks, and golfers, and baseball hitters constantly watch tape of themselves to analyze the small adjustments that can have big results. Actors and politicians analyze their face cues and body language.

**KEY CONCEPT**

**If you want to be a better communicator, listen and watch yourself communicating.**

If hearing yourself is just too weird, find or create some video of the league you are going to work and practice your communication STANDING UP in front of a computer or TV. With audio and video so accessible, there are multiple options to get better, as long as you are interested in putting in the practice.

# Coaches and Mentors

You don't have to go it alone. Find a mentor.

I believe you can have a mentor that doesn't even know you.

Throughout this book, I have talked about many of my mentors. Most of them I never met, but they influence my life and thinking. I never met Bruce Lee, but when I occasionally sit by his grave in Seattle, I think about big ideas and ask him for advice.

Look right in front of you. Who is a referee or umpire that you want to model yourself after? Who do you respect? When a game ends, who do the players go up to and thank? Who do they want to talk and joke with?

Find that ref or ump, and ask for their advice. Buy them lunch and ask them how they deal with tricky calls and tough players. What was their best day? What was their worst day? What was the biggest mistake they made in their first 15 games?

If that seems intimidating to you, make it even simpler: find refs and umps that you like and just COPY them. Grab a piece of paper, sit in the stands and watch.

No one is all good, and no one is all bad. Superstar refs that look invincible have flaws. Refs that look like they don't belong taught me a lot about communication and confidence.

**Borrow *one good thing* from every ref you watch and work with, and you will be a better ref.**

When I first got started, flag football was easier for me, but I struggled mightily with softball. So I just copied our best softball umps. One in particular, Will, just appeared one day, as if he walked out of the cornfield in *Field of Dreams*.

Everyone loved Will, and he had some mannerisms that just made sense to me. He was laid-back and simply unshakable when it came to arguments and conflicts. Everything he did just seemed easy. I copied as much as I could from him: the way I announce a strike on the corner of the plate, and the cool way he picked up a bat—not by bending over, but by stepping on the end of the barrel and then handing it to a player. One day, he was gone. He didn't show up for a shift, and we never heard from him again.

I never asked Will to be my mentor, but he was. I hope his best traits live on every time I ump softball.

When we started kickball back in 2005, we were lucky to have Lawrence, aka "the Godfather of Kickball", join the Underdog team. Lawrence was by far one of the best Social Refs I have ever seen. His communication, his teaching style, his movement, and his sense of humor puts him in the Social Ref Hall of Fame.

When I started umping kickball–and struggling there, too–I just started copying Lawrence as much as I could.

Of course, there were certain things that he could get away with, especially when it came to jokes and raw enthusiasm for the game, but I borrowed in small pieces to get better.

When I watched how Lawrence dealt with close and controversial calls with a laugh and a smile, I got better. We would talk about these situations after a game, or on long car rides between Underdog Portland and Seattle. Any way you slice it, he was my kickball mentor.

Nick, who coined the phrase, "*are they questioning you or asking a question?*" has been with Underdog for 16 years. His technique and mechanics are always flawless. When I was first struggling with making my signals and motion look more like a ref, I was lucky enough to just be able to work with him and copy his traits week after week.

Your mentor doesn't have to be Obi-Wan Kenobi, muttering inspirational quotes in your ear. They can just be someone who has a couple of really good ideas that you want to learn. In the Social Ref world, sacrifice a little originality to build a better system.

Those first few games where you are stumbling around and just trying to keep your head above water might feel really confusing and lonely. Everyone has had them, though, and everyone must go through them, just like the first time you fell off your bike, or scraped up mom's car when you were learning how to park.

**Borrow from great people, because the great ones never seem to mind.**

Borrow their techniques, their scripts, their sounds, their jokes and comebacks, or their style. Borrow the way they prep themselves before the game even starts. The way they always seem to have a "back-up bag" with extra clothes and snacks. Borrow their routines, their movement patterns, and habits. Borrow the best and leave their worst behind.

Great writers copy other writers when they start. Great musicians and directors do the same. See borrowing as a sign of respect, and find a mentor to borrow from. In many cases, they are staring you right in the face if you pay attention. If someone has already figured out the best way to announce info, then just copy them. Ask for help, ask for advice, take them to lunch, watch them ref from the stands, but formal or informal, try and find a mentor.

# People and Progress

Wherever you are in your reffing journey, don't get lost in complexity.

Some ideas will be tough—it took me a long time to understand the infield fly rule and make it a habit. I wish there was some shortcut or hack for you to borrow, but you might just have to build the habit of looking at the players on base, and knowing the outs. . . **every single play**.

You will have penalties, calls and rulings, rule books, signals, gear, clickers, flags, score books, and whistles. You may have tests to take, you may have videos to watch. You may have charts to fill out or clinics to attend. In all of that complexity, try and remember one more simple idea:

**At the end of the day, you are communicating with people.**

KEY CONCEPT

Communication, information, hustle, engagement, your book cover, your defusion skills—they are made for people. You are not talking to a computer program or a robot. We spend so much time talking about brain instincts and reactions because they involve *people*.

These are people who are scared, confused, nervous, new, angry, tired, upset, hyped-up, and have backgrounds and experiences that you probably will never know. They have amazing stories, and unique perspectives.

If you stink at communication, like many of us do, you can practice and get better. You can work on it like a muscle. No one is born a great communicator, or a genius.

Bill Gates dropped out of Harvard, but he spent hundreds of hours at a computer, learning and practicing. Albert Einstein couldn't get a teaching job for 2 years after he graduated, so he ended up working at a patent office. Imagine seeing everyone's best ideas and systems coming across your desk for review day after day. It probably starts to impact the way you think and communicate about the world. All those patent applications might have been Einstein's Sandbox.

The great ones deal with complexity, but find a way to simplify things so everyone can understand—like Dr. Seuss. Good teachers always seem to simplify complex ideas.

**It is always simplicity that makes great social refs, never complexity.**

KEY CONCEPT

If this all seems too much, or out of reach, if you have always been an introvert, or shy, or lousy at communication, and if you have never reffed one game, I assure you, it is all possible. Communication habits and instincts get better with time. Others have already done it. We know their stories, we know what works. Great umps and refs built this communication system, and now the system will help build you into a great official and communicator.

Maybe your Social Reffing career is actually a Sandbox for something else bigger you are meant to do in life. Maybe you are meant to be a professor, a CEO, a leader, or even President. Maybe the communication and defusion skills you will learn and make into habits will stick with you for challenges bigger than a flag football game.

**You might find being a Social Ref MORE rewarding if it does not come easy to you at first.**

The best Social Refs we have ever seen make mistakes. They make *more* mistakes. They fail often, and they fail quick, because they default to being proactive.

Sometimes if reffing is too easy, people are gone fast. There is no growth, no learning, no reward, and no personal satisfaction.

If it's hard at first, and you struggle—you freeze up, blow a call, write down a score wrong, and trip over a cone and fall on your face—if you can power through those things, you might find a fulfillment and satisfaction on the other side that you were not expecting.

It's not about power, or control, or being right, or winning the argument, or being in charge.

**It's the idea of "True Confidence": never having to worry about changing someone else's opinion. Never having to *say* that you are right, or *tell* someone else that they are wrong.**

It's the satisfaction of knowing how hard it is to do the 5 jobs well and still fade into the background. It's the happiness and enjoyment of a job well done, of being a leader, and helping others have fun.

One of our best refs, Nicholas, tells two stories about his Social Ref path with Underdog. The first is when he spent the first 2 hours of his very first shift learning a different craft: shoveling snow. Imagine going through all of the videos and education and practice, then showing up to a football field nervous to ref for the first time and seeing it covered in snow.

Sometimes you just have to shovel snow. . . to help own the field.

The second story he tells is about his certification. After a set amount of games we do an on-field test to make sure that a ref is ready proceed to the next level. In one of his games, Nicholas had a rough go—a playoff game that spiraled out of control towards the end in a classic melt-down fashion. The original culprit?

He had written down a 1 instead of a 2 for an extra point, and told both teams the wrong score. Things went downhill from there and he failed the certification.

I was on the field with him that day, and gave the failing grade. He was not ready. . . yet. Even though he had a tough day, you could see in his eyes that he was going to be a great Social Ref. The tough game, the scoreboard problem, and the rough ending made him better that day, because he wanted to get better.

My mentor Barrett often tells me: Everything tends to happen to everybody; it's how people respond that makes the difference.

Nicholas wasn't the only ref to have a test that day. A second ref did, and guess what—he also failed. Except he complained, said we were wrong, and quit a week later.

Nicholas said to himself, "*I need to get better to make sure that game info problem never happens again*," and he did. Fast-forward three years, and he is a supervisor, a mentor, and an amazing Social Ref across multiple sports.

If it's tough at first, you might find that things actually get *easier* after those first 15 games.

You're probably going to have your share of mistakes and goof-ups. If you don't, then you probably aren't trying very hard. How are you going to respond when they happen?

Blame the players? Talk about how silly the rulebook is? Say that reffing just isn't for you?

It's okay if you decide that after you try 15 games. Reffing always looks easier in slow-motion on TV when someone else is getting yelled at.

But if you find it tough, or rough, or close to impossible, try one idea:

**Keep reffing. . .**

Take a deep breath, shake it off, explain what you saw, and get to the next play.

Defuse, joke, pivot, smile, inform, break momentum; do what you can to get out of a tense moment and on with the game.

Sometimes that's the way games go, and often that's the way life goes.

Avoid the impulse to be perfect, remember no one is 100% correct, have fun at a path that is seldom taken, and keep reffing.

You will learn to enjoy what you find on the other side of a tough game and a really tough day: the realization that you actually did a pretty good job, that you're still here, and another game with new opportunities and challenges is waiting for you tomorrow.

## FAREWELL: THE FOUL BALL

It's opening day of spring softball in Seattle, 2018.

Walking up to the field, I notice there aren't even bases in the ground.

*"Crap."* I'm early, but not early enough.

The day is choppy—like most opening days—and just for fun, it rains off-and-on throughout the first couple of games.

There are questions about rosters, comments about shirts, confusion from new players about the number of fielders, and even a triple play. Not bad.

The most amazing part comes in Game Three. The team wearing bright red shirts has runners on second and third and their batter hits a ball down the third base line.

And man, is it close. . .

The ball is maybe 5 inches foul, but it's clearly foul.

"**FOUL BALL!**" I yell at the top of my lungs, with a little bit of special sauce.

I turn to my left and see the red team captain smiling and clapping.

"*I love it!*" he yells loudly at me, flashing me the thumbs up signal.

Even after 18 years, my instincts are still a bit defensive.

"*Is he being sarcastic? Did I do something wrong?*"

Turns out he is being real and genuine. It's one of those rare things—a COMPLIMENT!

He is literally applauding me for making a foul ball call **that takes 2 runs away from his team**.

Really, he is applauding something else: engagement, movement and communication. *Giving a crap.*

I am making the foul call standing on top of the third base bag, right in front of his dugout. I don't even remember moving there; my Ref Brain just took over.

The Red captain loses two runs, but applauds the effort and the action, even when the call doesn't go his way.

Everyone notices effort. Everyone notices when you end up in a spot that most refs and umps never do.

Everyone notices when you are trying as hard as they are trying, and you are looking out for them.

As luck would have it, Jay came out of retirement to work an emergency softball shift just as I was finishing up this book. We talked at lunch about his Sunday games, and he told the story of a rule argument from a "passionate" captain.

"*It's okay, the rule is confusing. Check it out when you get a chance*," Jay told the captain during the game in a natural defuser pivot.

After the game was over, with the rulebook on his smart phone, the captain came back to Jay and said:

"*Thank you.*"

For making great calls? For umping fair and enforcing the rules?

Nope.

He said, "*Thanks for not embarrassing me in front of my teammates when I didn't know the rule.*"

After all these years, Jay is still a great Social Ref. Because the people are more important than the rulebook.

We have talked a ton about conflict, communication, and arguments. It might seem like reffing is nothing but yelling and problems all day long. It's really not as bad as it sounds. We didn't want to scare you, just try and prepare you.

The truth is, I have loved every minute of it, even when both teams left the field hating my calls and my guts. Reffing is a rare thing. **You are busting your butt to make sure someone else has fun**, and gets a fair shake. You ref in service to others, so they can play, while you are at work.

You may never hear applause or get compliments for a really great call. There will be those great moments when you change the future for the better and you are the ONLY one who notices. When the Ref Brain is switched on, you will start to feel those moments in your gut.

Reffing teaches us two big ideas about life:

1. **How you respond when things go wrong, not just when things go right.**

2. **Sometimes you can do everything right, and everyone will still think you are wrong.**

Remember, Coach Coats was totally right about that crazy chess move. I just didn't play chess again for another 10 years. Joe was 100% right on his Volcano Call, but because of the delivery, he lost credibility with the players. I was right to stop and check on the guy who fell down on the sidewalk, and maybe TechnoGuy was right to honk at me because I slowed down in front of him. You technically made the perfect "by the book" call on Doug with your hat in the end zone, and you *still* broke his heart.

**You have to be better than just "being correct" to become a great communicator and a Social Ref.**

Over time, you will be able to change the future. You will see patterns, sense profiles, know where the ball is going and feel your next potential problem. Your Ref Brain will start to notice when things are off and help fix them *before* they spiral out of control. Give your Ref Brain a chance by working on your switchboard.

If you were to get thrown out on a field as a ref 15 minutes from now, and you had no rulebook, no equipment, and no training, what would you do?

You could blame the situation, say you're new, and ask for sympathy because of the poor hand you were dealt.

Or you could just start moving. You could engage with the game and "hide behind hustle". You could communicate with teams, and learn very quickly what info they need. You could ask for help. You could do tiny favors, and you could collect thank you's and build credibility.

You could announce penalties and fouls like someone who understands how it feels to be criticized in front of friends, like someone who assumes that people are trying their best.

People might like or hate the calls you make, but they really care more about the way you make them.

It's the delivery that makes the joke. And it's the communication that makes a Social Ref.

So I will finish, asking for your help:

Help us change the idea of what a "Ref" means to people. Help us turn the symbol of a ref uniform from "that's who tells me what I did wrong," to, "that ref helps me learn, understand, and have MORE fun."

**Help us with good calls, made with your great communication.**

Now as my dad used to say:

*"Call 'em like you see 'em."*

. . . and don't forget to have fun.

**Shawn D. Madden**
*Ambassador of Fun*
Seattle, Washington—August 13th, 2018

*www.SocialRef.net*

SCRIPT SHEET

# Starter Script Sheet Summary

1. A player tells you, *"Oh man, that's the worst call I have ever seen!"*

_____

_____

_____

2. A player asks, *"Why didn't you make that call? Everyone saw it!"*

_____

_____

_____

3. A coach says, *"Are you sure about that rule, ref???"*

_____

_____

_____

4. What is your CCS? What are the components and order? When will you say it?

_____

_____

_____

5. What will be your apology phrase when you know you made a mistake?

_____

_____

_____

6. What pivot will you use to avoid over-explaining your call?

_____

_____

_____

7. Who is your Kryptonite on the field? How will you respond?

_____

_____

_____

8. What will your response be when players say you missed a call?

_____

_____

_____

9. What is your go-to defuser joke?

_____

_____

_____

10. What is a new player phrase or script you will can use?

_____

_____

_____

Additional notes for the Script Sheet:

_____

_____

_____

_____

_____

_____

_____

_____

_____

_____

_____

_____

# Key Concept Summary

## All Key Concepts throughout the Book

- It's not the calls, it's YOUR communication.

- Climb down off the pedestal. Meet the players where they are. Nobody came to watch you ref.

- If you have to say you are in charge, you aren't in charge— you're just acting like a jerk.

- CAP is built into the game because conflict is built into the DNA of the job.

- Are players questioning you, or asking a question?

- There are at least 3 versions of every game:

  The First Game that the home team and their fans see.

  The Second Game that the away team and their fans see.

  And the **Third Game** that you the ref need to see to do your job!

- If you're watching the ball fly through the air, you are normally watching the wrong thing.

- You need to trigger decisions with your feet first.

- When you first start, you won't need more knowledge— you will need more movement.

- You need to learn and know the rules. Then you need to move past the rule book.

- Most people decide to ref and don't realize that there are actually 5 jobs.

- Start by building the key habit of giving out game info to "become the scoreboard."

- The most important question is, *"What game info do the players need right now, even if they haven't asked?"*

- It is *really hard* to be too loud in a rec league game.

- It is almost impossible to repeat the core game info too many times.

- Most sports have at least one sequence that is the core priority for every play. We call this the Core Communication Sequence or CCS.

- Remembering is never a system. It's just something you tell yourself when you don't actually have a system.

- Hearing everything because you're into the game is good. Responding to everything you hear is really, really bad, and will just distract you from the core habit.

- If you start using your habits and systems only when games are tough and close, you will quickly find you have no system to use.

- All defusion starts with a basic idea: first, avoid making things worse.

- Over-explaining a call that no one likes is an escalator.

- Whether or not you saw the play, there is always a simple pivot: *"I will watch for it going forward."*

- There is always one simple start to breaking downward momentum: Stop the game. "Send the meal back."

- Be direct with YOU and YOUR when giving good news and compliments; be detached with the Historical Voice when giving bad news and explanations—things that feel like criticism.

- As a ref, humor always works best when used for defense—never to go on offense

- Lots of big arguments about penalties and fouls are really a part of a simple defense: "*I didn't do it on purpose.*"

- Sometimes your best call will be a simple warning.

- When in doubt, don't assume. . . let them know you heard it and saw it.

- A game ALWAYS feels unfair when you didn't get your full time.

- If players are arguing about rules and you are standing there watching, you are doing something wrong.

- If you want to be a better communicator, listen and watch yourself communicating.

- At the end of the day, you are dealing and communicating with people.

- It is always simplicity that makes great social refs, never complexity.

# Thank You's and Shout-Outs

Blake "Blammer" Madden

Nick Ferate, the First Reader

The Underdog Family

Dillion Kreider

Barrett Ersek

Carol Mayes

Jay Gilliand

Bruce Lee

Jim Rohn

Ed Hochuli

Mike Carey

Steve Pavlina

Mike Grabham

Perry Marshall

Shane Parrish (Farnam Street)

Ray Beauchamp

T. Kira Madden (Little Sis)

Bobby D. from Delaware

Seneca

Todd Moore

Malcolm Gladwell

Ryan Holiday

Brian Eno, "Thursday Afternoon"

Turtles

Montlake Public Library

"Babe"

Laurie Ruettimann

Jason Pollentier

"Tabbeltron"

"The Three Steven's": King, Pressfield, and Uncle

Every Ref and Ump that has worked a game with Underdog